HOW TO USE THIS GUIDE BOOK AND THE MAPS

The garden at Chatsworth covers 105 acres. While many of the famous features are not far from the house, if you explore further afield you will discover beautiful, peaceful and unusual parts [...] are welcome to picnic and play wherev[...]

The garden bears the marks of many of the [...] important eras in European garden design over the last 450 years. At the end of this book, from page 51, an illustrated history section builds up the layers of history and shows you what has survived from each period. It is worth glancing at this before you set out.

There are a number of different ways to find your way around:

EITHER **1**

USE THE MAP ON THE BACK COVER

which shows all the principal features and paths, to wander as you please. It also indicates the best paths for wheelchairs and pushchairs. ♿ ➡

OR **2**

FOLLOW THE FULL TOUR

which starts on page 4. Use the 'Finding your way' maps in the bottom right hand corners to see where you are and to direct you on your walk.
This covers everything in the book, so you can use the map on the back to leave and rejoin this tour.

OR **3**

FOLLOW THE FOUR SPECIAL TRAILS

which highlight different aspects of the garden. These are on the inside front and back covers and there is also a 'Discovering Paxton' map on page 26.

Orangery Borders
Emperor Fountain
Sunday music
Pinetum

The Duke
and Duchess
of Devonshire

Welcome to
the Garden

The 105 acre garden that surrounds this
house is one of the most fascinating and
beautiful historic landscapes in England.
Many generations of my family have
contributed to this place over five centuries,
sometimes with the help of outstanding
garden designers but often inspired by their
own taste and passion. Each generation has
respected the best of what came before but
they have also understood that a garden is a
living place which must change and grow,
and this philosophy continues today.

Nothing could be achieved in this garden
without the tireless efforts of the head
gardener, Ian Webster, and his team. It gives
all of us who live and work here great
pleasure that so many visitors come back
throughout the year to enjoy the changing
seasons. If this is your first visit, I hope you
will be inspired to return and see the garden
as it continues to evolve.

Devonshire

A POTTED FAMILY TREE

Over the last 450 years the garden at Chatsworth has evolved into the garden you see today. Some of its owners were content to enjoy it but not to alter it, others made such major changes as to transform the appearance of the garden completely. This guide book looks at what they did, why they did it and how their changes are reflected in the garden of today.

BESS OF HARDWICK
b. 1527 m. Sir William Cavendish
THE FIRST GARDEN IN 1617   Page 52

1618   1st EARL OF DEVONSHIRE
       William Cavendish b.1552

1626   2nd EARL OF DEVONSHIRE
       William Cavendish b.1590

1628   3rd EARL OF DEVONSHIRE
       William Cavendish b.1617

1684   4th EARL OF DEVONSHIRE
       William Cavendish b.1641
       1694 created
       1st DUKE OF DEVONSHIRE
       THE FORMAL GARDEN IN 1699   Page 54

1707   2nd DUKE OF DEVONSHIRE
       William Cavendish b.1673

1729   **3rd DUKE OF DEVONSHIRE**
       William Cavendish b.1698
       A TIME OF CHANGE, 1743   Page 56

1755   **4th DUKE OF DEVONSHIRE**
       William Cavendish b.1720
       THE LANDSCAPE GARDEN, c.1770   Page 58

1764   5th DUKE OF DEVONSHIRE
       William Cavendish b.1748

1811   **6th DUKE OF DEVONSHIRE - 'Bachelor Duke'**
       William Spencer Cavendish b.1790
       THE CONQUEST OF NATURE - 1858   Page 60

1858   7th DUKE OF DEVONSHIRE
       William Cavendish b.1808

1891   8th DUKE OF DEVONSHIRE
       Spencer Compton Cavendish b.1833

1908   9th DUKE OF DEVONSHIRE
       Victor Cavendish b.1868

1938   10th DUKE OF DEVONSHIRE
       Edward Cavendish b.1895

1950   **11th DUKE OF DEVONSHIRE**
       Andrew Cavendish b.1920
       AND THE GARDEN TODAY   Page 62

2004   12th DUKE OF DEVONSHIRE
       Peregrine Cavendish b.1944

A TOUR OF THE GARDEN

There are three entrances to the garden

FROM THE HOUSE

As you leave the house by way of the Orangery shop you will see the Orangery Borders in front of you. On your left is Flora's Temple.

FROM THE LOWER GARDEN ENTRANCE

From the car park you walk up a ramp and through Flora's Temple. To your right is the Orangery shop with the Orangery Borders extending out from it.

FROM THE STABLES ENTRANCE

On entering the garden, turn right towards the house. At the bottom of the path you will see Flora's Temple on your right and the Orangery Borders to your left.

THE ORANGERY BORDERS
c.1960s

The borders are planted with annuals and herbaceous plants.

Near the house blues and whites predominate and 'Iceberg' roses are backed by clipped and bound Irish yews (*Taxus baccata* 'Fastigiata'). The borders across the Broad Walk are backed by hard-pruned red oaks (Quercus rubra) and are planted in yellows, oranges and reds.

THE ORANGERY (now a shop)

Built in 1827 for the 6th Duke to house his newly introduced *Rhododendron arboreum*, *Altingia excelsa* and orange trees from the Empress Josephine's garden at Malmaison. The empress, who was Napoleon's wife, employed the artist Redouté to record her collection.

BERLIN TAZZA

This massive granite vase was acquired by the 6th Duke who had a great passion for stone.

MOLOSSIAN HOUNDS

The stone dogs on each side of the steps leading from the borders are copies of the Molossian Hound, or Dog of Alcibiades, a classical sculpture now in the British Museum.

LOOK FOR

BLUE AND WHITE BORDERS

Anchusa azurea **'Feltham Pride'**
July. Electric blue flowers.

Lilium regale **'Album'**
August. Sprays of white scented flowers flushed with purple.

Delphinium **'Summer Skies'**
June/July. Pale blue spikes.

Crambe cordifolia
July. White 'drifts of smoke'.

ORANGE & RED BORDERS

Lobelia **'Cardinalis'**
Late summer. Tall with dark red leaves and intense red flowers.

Crocosmia **'Lucifer'**
July-September. Orange.

Dahlia **'Moonfire'**
July-September. Burnt orange.

Flora's Temple was built in 1695 by the 1st Duke as a bowling green house, designed as an imitation of a classical temple. The temple was originally built in what is now the West Garden; it was moved to its present position in about 1760.

FLORA

This sculpture of the classical Goddess of Flowers, probably by Caius Gabriel Cibber (1630-1700), has moved several times. This was originally the centre-piece of 'Flora's Garden', an area laid out by the 1st Duke in the 1690s. In the engraving by Kip and Knyff, page 54, Flora can be seen standing where the Emperor Fountain is today with the Bowling Green House to the left.

In about 1760 she was moved into the relocated Bowling Green House, which was then named Flora's Temple. In 1813 the 6th Duke moved her to his new French Garden, now the Rose Garden, but in 1993 she was returned to her temple.

LIMESTONE BOULDER

Nearly 250,000 years ago, this boulder was deposited nearby by a glacier moving south from Pindale near Castleton.

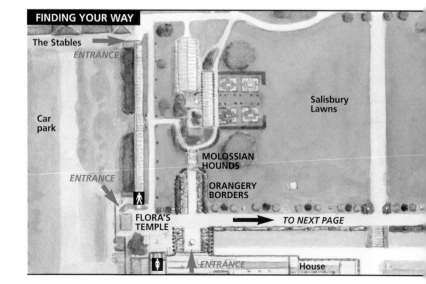

FINDING YOUR WAY

The Stables
ENTRANCE

Car park

ENTRANCE

FLORA'S TEMPLE

Salisbury Lawns

MOLOSSIAN HOUNDS

ORANGERY BORDERS

TO NEXT PAGE

ENTRANCE   House

5

THE BROAD WALK
1820s

The 6th Duke's Broad Walk is a third of a mile long and stretches south from Flora's Temple.

It runs parallel to the 6th Duke's North Wing and the East Front of the house. The path continues between the Salisbury Lawns and the South Lawn and on through a beech avenue ending at the top of a rise with Blanche's Vase silhouetted on the skyline. About 100 years ago, the row of golden Irish yews, (*Taxus baccata* 'Aureomarginata') and green Irish yews, (*Taxus baccata* 'Fastigiata'), replaced the monkey puzzle trees which had been recently introduced into Britain when the Broad Walk was created.

STATUES
19th century English copies commissioned by the 6th Duke to replace the 1st Duke's copies of antique originals.

THE LION STEPS
Leading down to the South Lawn the steps are named after the copies of the Medici Lions placed here in the 1820s. The slope on either side replaced an unfenced drop. In the 5th Duke's time, the politician Charles James Fox, racing down the hill, inadvertently fell over this drop and broke his leg.

BLANCHE'S VASE
The vase was commissioned by the 6th Duke in memory of his beloved niece, born Blanche Howard, who married his heir William Cavendish. She died in 1840 at the age of 28 having borne five children.

When 'Capability' Brown was working for the 4th Duke in the 1760s, he destroyed the formal terraces, with their parterres and fountains, and replaced them with featureless lawns. *See overleaf.*

Since then these five acres of grass, then called the Great Slope, have remained unchanged. Now, as then, a rich variety of wild flowers, heather, sedges and fifteen different species of moss grow on the lawn. Some of the wild flowers are listed on the right.

◆ *Watch out for slippery patches after rain.*

LOOK FOR

- Bird's-foot trefoil
- Cat's ear
- Field woodrush
- Harebell
- Heath & Lady's bedstraw
- Knapweed
- Lady's mantle
- Lady's smock
- Milkwort
- Mouse-eared hawk weed
- Ox-eye daisy
- Selfheal
- Sorrel
- Speedwell
- Tormentil
- Yarrow
- Yellow mountain pansy

HOW WAS IT MAINTAINED ?

The late 18th century picture above shows deer grazing in the foreground. The grass might also have been scythed. When the deer were excluded in the early 19th century the grass was mown first by horse drawn mowers and then by motor mowers. In 1832 the first cylindrical blade lawnmower appeared. It had a 19 inch blade and was pushed or pulled.

Today it takes one man just over 7 hours to mow the lawns which took nearly 20 man days to scythe.

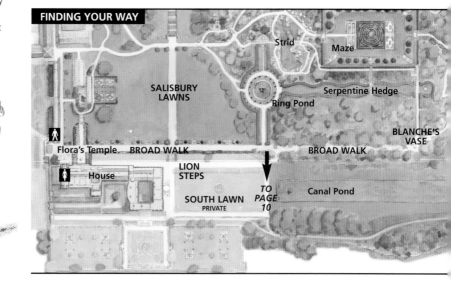

FINDING YOUR WAY

Strid
Maze
SALISBURY LAWNS
Serpentine Hedge
Ring Pond
BLANCHE'S VASE
Flora's Temple   BROAD WALK   BROAD WALK
House
LION STEPS
SOUTH LAWN PRIVATE   Canal Pond

TO PAGE 10

'CAPABILITY' BROWN
1716-83

After leaving school at 16, Lancelot Brown gained experience working in the vegetable garden of Sir William Loraine and rose to become head gardener at Stowe. His first major work on his own was at Croome Court in Worcestershire. Brown got on well with his aristocratic clients; he always saw 'great capabilities' in the landscapes he was asked to improve, thus earning the nickname 'Capability' Brown.

"...consult the Genius of the Place in all"

In early 18th century England, there was a slow evolution away from formality in garden design. The new fashion for the "appearance of beautiful nature" was to have a dramatic impact at Chatsworth. It reflected social changes and the English landowners' love of country life, but there were many other reasons for this rejection of the old style.

A MATTER OF TASTE
Taste and culture were crucially important to the 18th century ruling classes. To say that one had no taste was an insult. Houses, works of art, books and collections enhanced the owner's status and so did gardens.

EDUCATION AND ART
Most wealthy young Englishmen benefited from an education in the Classics and the opportunity to make the Grand Tour to Italy and the Continent. By the 1730s many treated the Tour as a debauched networking trip, but the more serious traveller returned with works of art, including 17th century landscape paintings by such artists as Claude Lorraine (above), depicting idyllic Italian landscapes with figures and buildings. It was not that these were necessarily seen as great paintings but were inexpensive souvenirs not affected by export restrictions. They also provided a visual model for the Arcadian landscapes of ancient Greece and Rome on which to base the new 'natural' look.

LITERATURE
Writers provided intellectual justification for the change in garden design. In a letter to Lord Burlington, 1731, Alexander Pope wrote *"All gardening is landscape painting"*, and in 1734 *"In all let Nature never be forgot ... consult the Genius of the Place in all"*. However John Evelyn had expressed similar views in the 17th century, so these were not entirely new ideas.

POLITICS
William Kent's Temple of Ancient Virtue, 1737, at Stowe (above), was based on the Temple of Vesta, Tivoli, and drawings from Palladio's *Quattro Libri*. It represented the ideal past and contrasted with the Temple of Modern Virtue, which was built as a ruin. Nearby, the Temple of British Worthies, adapted from a design for Chiswick, was a more blatant political statement.

STATUS
The landscape park grew out of the deer park, at a time when venison was a sign of wealth. The Enclosure Acts favoured wealthy landowners and enabled them to consolidate and enclose large areas. Roads were diverted and shelter belts of trees planted to ensure privacy; even villages were moved, the example here being Edensor.

AGRICULTURE
Not only did the landscape park provide sport and recreation but the grazing and forestry gave better economic returns than arable farming. After the destruction of forests and woodland during Cromwell's Commonwealth and with the expansion of the Navy, growing trees was considered patriotic as well as profitable for future generations.

SPORT
With the development of guns for sport, game shooting became a serious and popular pastime. Clumps of trees provided ideal cover for rearing game.

NEW SPECIES
The 18th century saw the introduction of new tree species into the country, from such places as the east coast of America. A detail of a plant list produced for Chatsworth by a nursery in Philadelphia, 1759 is shown above. It includes pines, cedars, catalpa, witch hazels and maples all to be sent to Chatsworth.

THE EVOLUTION OF THE NATURAL STYLE

In 1751, 'Capability' Brown, set up his own business as a designer and contractor offering a complete landscaping service. Despite poor health, he went on to create over 100 landscape parks using his formula of contoured expanses of turf stretching away from the house, past clumps of trees, flowering shrubs and a curving river or lake, before rising to a surrounding belt of trees. At Chatsworth, where the lie of the land was ideal for Brown's vision, it is estimated that his changes involved 25,000 man days of labour and a similar number of horse days.

BROWN'S LEGACY
A comparison between the engraving after Paul Sandby, 1775, and a present day photograph shows that, despite the re-introduction of a garden in the 19th century, many of the views created by Brown remain virtually unchanged.

A GRADUAL CHANGE
The slow evolution from formal to landscape gardens can be seen in these pictures. From the top: the formal garden, 1699; parterres to lawn, 1743; no division between garden and park, 1760s.

BOWOOD, WILTSHIRE
A classic Brownian landscape.

WHERE TO SEE MORE OF BROWN'S WORK

Before CHATSWORTH
Petworth, West Sussex
Burghley, Lincolnshire
Longleat, Wiltshire

After CHATSWORTH
Bowood, Wiltshire
Blenheim Palace, Oxfordshire
Richmond Park, Middlesex
St John's College, Cambridge
Syon Park, London
Sheffield Park, Sussex
Harewood, Yorkshire

THE SOUTH LAWN
PRIVATE

VERBASCUM
In front of the house, the arid gravel
path is punctuated by the self-seeding
Verbascum bombyciferum which has to
be kept under tight control.

Wagner Botanik, Wien 1828.

The South Lawn is on the oldest surviving flat terrace and dates
from the time of the Elizabethan house. The containing wall to the
west is of the same period.

Until 'Capability' Brown's changes, this terrace to the south of the
house was the Great Parterre, a pattern of intricate flower beds, hedges
and gravel paths. It was designed in 1694 by the leading gardeners of
the time, London and Wise, who also worked at Hampton Court Palace.
See the engraving (right) and 'The Formal Garden' (pages 36 & 37).
They ran the hundred acre Brompton Park Nursery, in Kensington,
which supplied Chatsworth with vast quantities of shrubs and trees,
including 12,000 hornbeams.

The eight Carrara marble statues and two urns were made by Francesco
Bienaimé for the 6th Duke in the 19th century.

PLEACHED LIMES
In 1952 the raised beds between the statues
were replaced with double rows of pleached
red-twigged limes (*Tilia platyphyllos* 'Rubra').
These are clipped in late July and it takes
4 men 10 days to complete the task. In the
1970s, it took 6 men 20 days to complete the
task using shears and secateurs.
'Pleached' means intertwined.

WINDOW BOXES

From October these massive iron boxes, introduced by the 6th Duke below the gilded window frames on the South Front, are planted with *Cheiranthus* 'Blood Red' which provide sheltered nesting for wagtails. They are followed by *Pelargonium* 'Vera Dillon' and 'Madame Crousse' which provide colour during the summer months.

SOUTH FRONT STAIRS

The detail of the 1699 engraving (above) shows William Talman's delicate curved flights of stairs complemented by Tijou's wrought iron balustrade. In 1837 Wyatville replaced Talman's stairs with the present stone steps which he copied from Chiswick House (below), one of the three London houses owned by the 6th Duke.

This fountain is fed by water flowing in a pipe from the base of the Cascade. The pressure resulting from the 50 foot drop provides the force for the display here. Triton and the sea horses were carved by Cibber whose statue of Flora is shown on page 5. Cibber worked here for four years (1688-91) but most of his outdoor statuary was replaced in the 19th century, so this example of his work is all the more precious. Three hundred years of buffeting by weather and water have had a sad effect on the sandstone.

LOOK FOR

OTHER CIBBER WORK AT CHATSWORTH

Statues at the top of the Great Stairs

Statues on either side of the Chapel altarpiece

Heads on the steps on the South Front

Statue of Flora

FINDING YOUR WAY

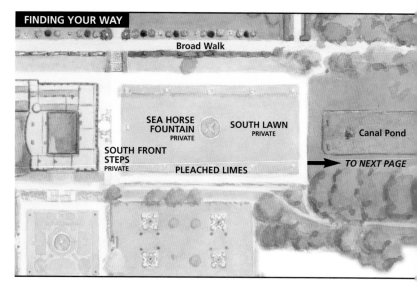

Broad Walk

SEA HORSE FOUNTAIN
PRIVATE

SOUTH LAWN
PRIVATE

Canal Pond

SOUTH FRONT STEPS
PRIVATE

PLEACHED LIMES

TO NEXT PAGE

THE CANAL POND
1702

The Canal Pond was dug in 1702. When Daniel Defoe came to Chatsworth he commented that a hill which had blocked the view had been "perfectly carried away" and replaced by this sheet of water 314 yards (287m) long.

Some genius set the Canal Pond a few inches higher than the South Lawn and when seen from the far end of the pond, the house appears to rise from the water.

The limes to the west of the Canal Pond were already big enough for Dr Johnson to walk under when he visited the 5th Duke and his Duchess, Georgiana, in 1784.

The grassy mound at the south-west end of the Canal Pond is the roof of an old ice house which was used until the 1920s to supply ice to the house kitchens.

WAR HORSE
1991, Bronze,
Dame Elisabeth Frink, 1930-93.
Placed with a view away from the house, towards Paine's Mill.

DAME ELISABETH FRINK
1992, Bronze, Angela Conner.
Placed in the garden by the 11th Duke and Duchess to commemorate their friendship with the artist.

UNVEILING OF THE WAR HORSE, 1992
Dame Elisabeth Frink and the Duchess of Devonshire.

THE WAR YEARS - PENRHOS COLLEGE
When war broke out in 1939, Penrhos College, a girl's school in North Wales, was taken over by the Ministry of Food. The 10th Duke arranged for the school to move into Chatsworth. Dormitories and classrooms were scattered throughout the house. The garden was used for sport and recreation. In the harsh winters the Canal Pond, being only 2 feet deep, made a perfect ice rink.

PAINE'S MILL, 1761-2
The mill was more than simply a replacement for the medieval mill which had been upstream. It was an important architectural feature, or 'eye-catcher', in 'Capability' Brown's new park, carefully positioned with its waterwheel visible from the end of the Canal Pond. It was a working mill until 1952.

THE EMPEROR FOUNTAIN
1843

When the Canal Pond was dug, part of the 1st Duke's scheme included the Great Fountain, which played to 94 feet (28m) and was supplied from what is now called Morton's Pond.

Although the Great Fountain was the highest in this country, the 6th Duke put Paxton's engineering skills into action (see overleaf) to create a new record-breaking gravity-fed fountain. When it became known that Czar Nicholas, Emperor of Russia, might visit Chatsworth the following year, 1844, the idea of welcoming the Czar with an even higher fountain than the one at Peterhof (see top right) appealed to the Duke. The work progressed at speed, continuing at night by the light of flares, and in six months it was finished. Alas, the Czar did not come, but the new fountain was named after him. It is on record as having reached the height of 296 feet (90m). In the picture on the right the jet would go off the top of this page.

PETERHOF, RUSSIA
The 6th Duke was a friend of Czar Nicholas I and had seen the 120 foot (37m) fountain at the Imperial Palace at Peterhof, when he attended the Czar's coronation in 1826. The record holder at the time was at Wilhelmshohe, near Kassel, reaching 190 feet (58m) (by 1844 it was out of order), the next was at St Cloud, 160 feet (49m), and the fountain at Versailles could only reach 90 feet (27m).

THE EMPEROR FOUNTAIN, c.1850
Lithograph, J.C.Bourne.

Near the fountain are two river gods, dating back to the 1st Duke's time, and attributed to Nadauld. They were restored in 2001.

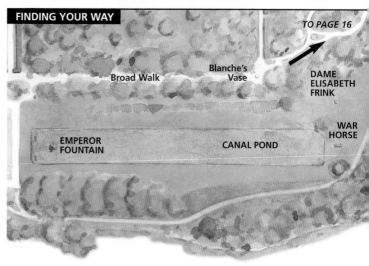

FINDING YOUR WAY

TO PAGE 16

Broad Walk — Blanche's Vase — DAME ELISABETH FRINK — WAR HORSE — EMPEROR FOUNTAIN — CANAL POND

WATER WORKS AT CHATSWORTH

Situated in a river valley in the heart of the Derbyshire Peak District, Chatsworth has always been blessed with a plentiful supply of water which has played an important role in the garden since the 1680s.

The 1st Duke's garden contained the Cascade, Canal Pond and the Willow Tree Fountain that can be seen today. If you look at the painting shown on page 37 you will see that there were also many other fountains. There was even a fountain in the Grotto inside the house; now known as the Diana Fountain, it still works. In the 1690s, piped water was used extensively within the house for water closets and for a bath for two people, with hot and cold water taps, unusual for this date.

Such water usage necessitated collecting and storing water and to do this three lakes were dug on the hill; the largest was what is now called the Swiss Lake. Relying on gravity, an elaborate system of ponds, watercourses and pipes led the water to where it was required. The Great Fountain was powered by the difference in the water level between it and the Great Fountain Pond, now Morton's Pond.

1. RAIN
Weather records kept at Chatsworth - 400ft (122m) above sea level - show that, on average, 34ins (87cm) of rain fall every year.

2. EMPEROR STREAM
Conduits were dug to fill the lakes with water draining off the moor. The Emperor Stream fills the Emperor Lake.

3. LAKES
The lakes hold over 80 million litres and can be seen from the Stand Wood walks. Some water drains down the Aqueduct and Cascade.

Water is also led down a direct pipe from the Emperor Lake to power the Emperor Fountain

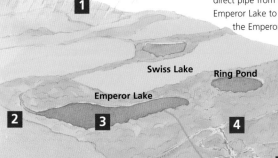

Swiss Lake

Ring Pond

Emperor Lake

Emperor pipe

It wasn't until the 6th Duke asked Paxton to engineer the Emperor Fountain that major changes were made to this gravity powered water system.

An additional lake, the Emperor, which covers nearly 8 acres, was dug to a depth of about 6ft (1.8m) and involved moving nearly 100,000 cubic yards (76,000m³) of soil, an immense task bearing in mind that this was before the advent of mechanical diggers. To feed the lake a 2.5 mile (4km) channel, the Emperor Stream, was dug across the moor to gather the rain that fell on the high ground. The pipe to the Emperor Fountain drops 400ft (122m) from the lake. In places trenches, up to 15ft (4.6m) deep, had to be cut through rock to maintain the gradient. The pipework for Paxton's works weighed about 220 tons. The water in the jet comes out with such staggering force that the valve has to be turned on very slowly to avoid shock damage. The system still works entirely by gravity.

11. EMPEROR FOUNTAIN
The Emperor Fountain is powered by a 16in (40cm) iron pipe direct from the Emperor Lake 400ft (122m) above. The Canal Pond drains into the river.

4. SOWTER STONE
Water from the Ring Pond flows over this stone and down to the Aqueduct, which can be seen to the left of the centre of the picture. Just to the right and above is the Cascade and to its left, in the trees, is the plume of the Emperor Fountain.

5. AQUEDUCT
Built by Paxton, c.1840, and based on one the 6th Duke had seen in Germany. The water continues downhill through Stand Wood and enters the garden above the Cascade Pond.

SOUGHS & PIPES
Stone water channels covered by slabs drain water down through the garden. Lead and the more recent iron pipes direct water under pressure to power the fountains.

6. CASCADE POND
The Cascade Pond, situated within the garden wall feeds water to the Cascade House and Cascade.

8. SEA HORSE FOUNTAIN
Water comes under pressure from the bottom of the Cascade.

7. CASCADE
Dropping down the Cascade most of the water drains into a 15in (38 cm) pipe which supplies the Sea Horse Fountain.

9. TULIP POND (Private)
From the Sea Horse Fountain the water is piped into this pond in the West Garden.

10. RIVER DERWENT
Finally the water enters the river, eventually to evaporate and return as rain.

A. REVELATION
Powered by water from a spur off the Emperor pipe.

2. TURBINE (Private)
Installed in 1893 and replaced in 1988, the turbine supplies electricity to the house. The water to drive the machinery comes from the Emperor Fountain pipe and is discharged through a pipe into the river.

B. WILLOW TREE POND
Fed from the Cascade Pond.

C. WILLOW TREE FOUNTAIN
Originally a copper tree, but replaced in the 19th century. This water trick is fed from the Willow Tree Pond.

D. STRID
Water flowing over the Wellington Rock, which is fed from the Cascade Pond and Trout Stream, goes into the Strid Pond.

E. RING POND
Fed from the Cascade Pond, Willow Tree Pond and Strid, the water then continues down to the Canal Pond. The pipe taking water direct from the Emperor Lake to the Emperor Fountain can be seen just below the surface of the pond.

THE AZALEA DELL
1900s

WILD GARDEN
Evelyn, wife of the 9th Duke, who lived here from 1907 to 1938, paid great attention to this area above the Azalea Dell and made massive plantings of spring flowers. The 'wild garden' was high fashion then and this was the ideal place for such a scheme. During the war of 1939-45 it was neglected and there is little left of her designs for her favourite part of the garden.

SPRING 1935
Traces of Evelyn's 'wild garden' were uncovered in the 1980s. The oak tree seen in this pictur lies where it fell and now has a large silver birch growing out of it.

Towards the end of May the azaleas are at their best and on a still day the smell of these sweet-scented shrubs is unforgettable. Azaleas are actually rhododendrons; they grow well here as the soil and conditions suit all but the tender varieties. The dell is planted with *Rhododendron* 'Ghent' and *Rhododendron luteum*. They are deciduous and colour brilliantly in the autumn.

EDENSOR SPIRE
The sudden glimpse of the church spire reminds you that you are in England rather than in the foothills of some mountainous country.

'HOSE IN HOSE'
Rhododendron 'Double Ghent' has double flowers.

The paths and much of the planting in the Ravine were the work of Evelyn, wife of the 9th Duke.

The south-facing bank of the Ravine is a wall of the purple flowered *Rhododendron ponticum,* discovered above the Black Sea in the early 1700s. Not a plant to be encouraged all over the garden because of its rampant and invasive nature, but on this bank it is impressive and worth keeping as a reminder of Victorian times when it was fashionable.

LOOK FOR

SPRING

Galanthus
Snowdrops.

Leucojum vernum
Spring snowflakes. Bulbous perennials with drooping bell-shaped flowers.

Saxifraga umbrosa 'London Pride'
A remnant of the alpine scree garden that was here previously.

Rhododendron 'Loderi King George'
June. Pink bud opens to white sweet-smelling flowers.

SUMMER

Gunnera manicata
Largest leaves of any garden plant. Tall spikes of tiny green-red flowers.

Osmunda regalis
The royal fern. The new growth of distinctive rust coloured fronds are produced in the centre of the plant.

AUTUMN

A wide variety of fungi can be seen.

WINTER

Mahonia 'Charity'
Evergreen. Fragrant yellow flowers from autumn to spring.

FINDING YOUR WAY

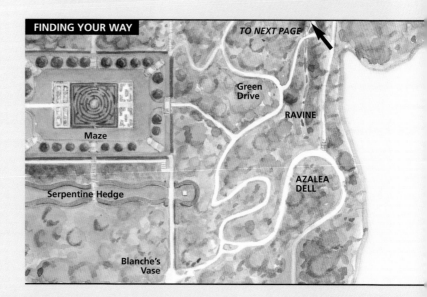

TO NEXT PAGE

Green Drive

RAVINE

Maze

AZALEA DELL

Serpentine Hedge

Blanche's Vase

THE TROUGH WATERFALL
1997

The piped overflow from the Grotto Pond was transformed into a waterfall in 1997 using stone drinking troughs which were lying about in the fields.

They are all shapes and sizes including one like a giant cup. The 13 troughs are slightly tipped so that the water flows over the lower edge of each into the one below.

LOOK FOR

Lysochiton americanus
Skunk cabbage.
Spike of green flowers hooded by bright yellow spathe.

Kalmia latifolia
Calico bush.
Glossy evergreen with clusters of pink flowers, in July, formed from distinctive crimped buds.

Primula
Candelabra primroses.
June - August.
Pyramid of flowers borne on a stalk.

Camassia
A show of blue flowers from May to July.

Iris pseudocarus
Yellow iris that thrives in damp shady places.

BIRDS

In this secluded part of the garden there is such a diversity of habitats within a relatively small area that it attracts a wide variety of birds. Some live here all the year round, some come for the summer months while others are passing through on their way to distant destinations.

LOOK FOR

ALL YEAR

POCHARD
A distinctive duck; the male has a rusty-red head and black shoulders. Nests in the reeds.

TUFTED DUCK
Since its introduction to Britain in the mid 19th century it has become our commonest diving duck.

MALLARD
Familiar dabbling duck. Feeds on the surface of the water.

COOT
Has an area of bare skin above its beak - hence "bald as a coot". Nests in the reeds.

SUMMER

SPOTTED FLYCATCHER
Perches on branches before darting out to capture its prey. Winters in central Africa.

OCCASIONALS

BUZZARD
Circles effortlessly, using updraughts, while looking for its prey of small mammals.

THE BIRDS OF GREAT BRITAIN
1862-73. John Gould. 55 x 37cm.
Hand coloured lithographs, after drawings mostly by Josef Wolf, give a detailed record of the birds that were present in this country over a century ago.

ALSO

Goldcrest	Tawny owl
Hawfinch	Goshawk
Long-tailed tit	Raven
Nuthatch	Thrush
Great crested grebe	Robin
Little grebe	Wren

GROTTO POND
The extra walk is amply rewarded when the pond reflects the autumn colours; especially those of the silver birch along the shore.

The Grotto was built in 1798 for Georgiana, the famous wife of the 5th Duke. The bandstand was added by her son the 6th Duke. The pond itself dates back further and was once an ancient fish pond. This area was once part of Sherwood Forest and near the Grotto are the remains of some ancient oaks. In the Old Park nearby some of the oaks are over 700 years old.

The Norfolk reeds at the edge of the pond provide an ideal habitat for birds and toads.

LOOK FOR

Rhododendron luteum
Azaleas are rhododendrons and this azalea's leaves colour brilliantly in autumn.

Hamamelis x intermedia 'Pallida'
After their autumn display witch hazels bear bright yellow clusters of flowers on their bare branches.

Pinus wallichiana
Introduced into Britain in 1823, the Bhutan pine has an attractive blue-green foliage and orange-pink bark.

ALEXANDER POPE IN HIS GROTTO
This 1725 drawing by William Kent shows a grotto being used for contemplation. Grottoes, often decorated with minerals, pebbles or shells, became fashionable in the 18th century. These cave-like structures were popular in Renaissance Italy and harked back to the civilisations of ancient Greece and Rome. Some grotto owners in England even employed 'Druids' to occupy them to add to their mystical atmosphere or sometimes, at less expense, a stuffed hermit.

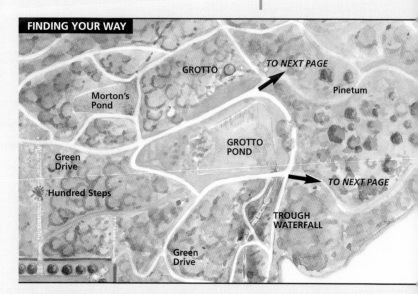

FINDING YOUR WAY

Morton's Pond

GROTTO

TO NEXT PAGE

Pinetum

Green Drive

Hundred Steps

GROTTO POND

TO NEXT PAGE

TROUGH WATERFALL

Green Drive

COLLECTING MANIA

Like many of his contemporaries the 6th Duke was an enthusiastic collector of plants and sent expeditions all over the world. These were often led by Chatsworth gardeners until two of them, Robert Wallace and Peter Banks, were drowned in the Columbia River having crossed Canada and the Rockies.

Plants whose names include the specific epithets such as *cavendishii*, *devoniana, burlingtonia* or *paxtonii,* were introduced by members of the family and bear witness to the 6th Duke's and Paxton's quest to find new species and the high regard in which they were held in horticultural circles.

In 1824, David Douglas was sent out by the Horticultural Society to collect plants from the north-west of America. He discovered and introduced many of the conifers found in Britain today. These new introductions became very fashionable throughout the 19th century.

In his Handbook the 6th Duke wrote "That is the Douglas pine, the pride of California: in 1829 it came down in Mr Paxton's hat, and in 1845 it is 35 feet high".

PHYTANTHOZA ICONOGRAPHIA
Weinmann, Regensburg, 1737-45
An early flora containing 1,025 engraved plates by various artists.

GENUS PINUS
Lambert, London, 1828-37
104 coloured lithographic plates. This one shows *Pinus strobus,* the Weymouth pine.

One of the consequences of this collecting mania was that the design of gardens and parks began to change. Humphry Repton, 'Capability' Brown's 'successor', started introducing areas for growing flowers into his landscape gardens so that these new introductions could be seen.

This is the farthest point of the garden and contains rarities such a *Chamaecyparis obtusa,* the Hinoki cypress, one of the most revered of the five sacred trees of Japan.

In 1829, the 6th Duke enclosed eight acres of the park at the south end of the garden to make this Pinetum, which contains approximately 200 conifers. Many of the conifers he planted were new introductions to this country. Over a hundred years passed with no change but in 1956 a few more conifers were added:

Abies veitchii, and *A. firma;*
Chamaecyparis pisifera 'Squarrosa',
C. lawsoniana 'Stewartii' and
C. nookatensis 'Pendula';
Picea pungens 'Glauca';
Sequoia sempervirens.

The old oaks are the north-western outliers of Sherwood Forest. There is a superb view over the ha-ha to the Old Park, river and New Piece Wood.

PINUS PEUCE
The Macedonian pine was introduced into Britain in 1864. This one is described as a champion tree as, at over 140 feet (42m), it is the highest tree of its kind in the country.

Many trees were blown down in the gale of 1962. In 1985 sixty conifers were planted here and some *Sorbus vilmorinii*, valuable for their pink berries which cheer up a dark November day.

LOOK FOR

Some of the 6th Duke's original plantings can still be seen:

Sequoiadendron giganteum
Wellingtonia.
Discovered in America in 1852, where it has lived to well over 3,000 years old. Named after the Duke of Wellington who died in the year it was discovered.

Pinus contorta
Shore pine. The lodgepole pine is a variety of this tree and gets its name from the central pole supporting Native American lodges, or tepees.

Pinus ponderosa
Western yellow pine. It was from this pine that tree-ring dating was developed.

Pinus mugo
Mountain pine.

Pinus strobus
Weymouth pine. Introduced in 1705.

Juniperus chinensis
Scale like leaves and attractive bluish berries.

Pseudotsuga menziesii
Douglas fir. Introduced in 1827.

PICEA BREWERIANA
Brewer's weeping spruce, a sad-looking droopy tree.

SPRING
The many different varieties of conifers are surrounded by a carpet of bluebells.

FINDING YOUR WAY

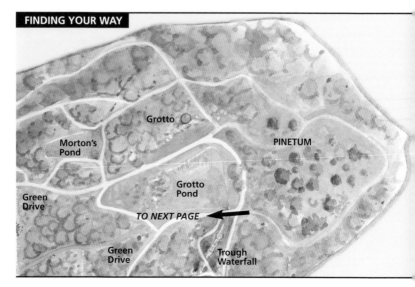

Grotto

Morton's Pond

PINETUM

Green Drive

Grotto Pond

TO NEXT PAGE

Green Drive

Trough Waterfall

THE ARBORETUM 1835
& THE HUNDRED STEPS 1980s

Paxton began work on the Arboretum in the 1830s. Forty acres were planted with 1,670 species arranged as a systematic succession of trees in accordance with botanical classification.

Few traces of this survive and what we call the Arboretum today is an area where trees and shrubs are dominant. Recently much of the area has been cleared of the invasive *Rhododendron ponticum* revealing hidden paths and even a statue.

Following the broad path northwards you will see paths leading up to Morton's Pond and further on a rediscovered altar marks the top of the Hundred Steps. Soon the Trout Stream appears on your right and leads into the Spectacles.

MORTON'S POND
In 1858 this secluded pond high up in the garden was called the Great Fountain Pond and supplied the gravity-fed Great Fountain lower down in the Canal Pond.

THE HUNDRED STEPS
To the right of the steps can be seen the remains of the flue leading from the Great Conservatory to the chimney hidden out of sight in Stand Wood.
On either side of the steps are two lines of Cypress oak, *Quercus robur* 'Fastigiata'. On a smaller scale are the sweet-smelling pheasant's eye narcissus (*N. poeticus* var. *recurvus*). At the top is a Roman altar purchased by the 6th Duke.

TROUT STREAM AND THE SPECTACLES
A shallow stream taking water from the moor meanders beside the Green Drive in the north-east part of the garden. On its journey, which at times appears to be uphill, it passes through two small ponds called the Spectacles, before dropping down a small waterfall near the Summer House and into the Jack Pond, where Revelation opens and closes (page 39).

THE HUNDRED STEPS
Half way down is a monkey puzzle tree or Chile pine, *Araucaria araucana*, a great favourite with the Victorians. Although discovered in 1782, it wasn't until 1844 that the first viable seeds arrived in Britain.

The Maze was planted in 1962 on the site of Paxton's Great Conservatory which was demolished in 1920 (see overleaf). Now all that can be seen are the sandstone foundation walls. Designed by Dennis Fisher, house comptroller, the maze required ,209 English yews (*Taxus baccata*). Gravel replaced the original grass paths as they got worn and gave clues as to the correct route. In case you don't get to the middle, it is marked by a weeping willow-leaved ear (*Pyrus salicifolia* 'Pendula').

LUPINS AND DAHLIAS
In early summer the lupins are a mass of colour. Then, from August until the first frost, the dahlias, introduced in the late 18th century from Mexico, take over.

HUMAN SUNDIAL, 1990
t the north end of the Great Conservatory arden is a large flat stone. Stand on the elevant month and your shadow falls on the me of day, and allows for summer and inter time.

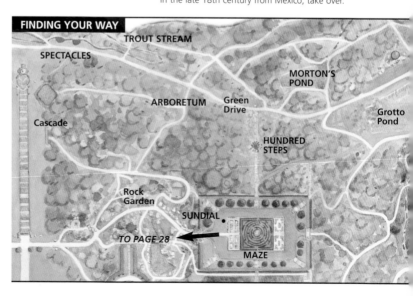

FINDING YOUR WAY

TROUT STREAM

SPECTACLES

MORTON'S POND

ARBORETUM   Green Drive

Grotto Pond

Cascade

HUNDRED STEPS

Rock Garden

SUNDIAL

TO PAGE 28

MAZE

SIR JOSEPH PAXTON

1803-65

Joseph Paxton worked in the garden of the Horticultural Society, which was adjacent to Chiswick Villa, one of the 6th Duke's London properties. The Duke was so impressed by Paxton's abilities that he made him Head Gardener at Chatsworth in 1826. Paxton's drive and efficiency soon brought results. His skill as a botanist is shown in the Pinetum and later in the Arboretum. Plant collecting expeditions were sent all over the world on behalf of the Duke (see pages 20-22). Paxton's most familiar work at Chatsworth is the Emperor Fountain, but his crowning achievement was the Great Conservatory. This was the forerunner to his famous Crystal Palace, built for the Great Exhibition, 1851. A self-taught man of wide interests, Paxton became a Director of the Midland Railway in 1848. He was knighted after the success of the Crystal Palace and in 1854 was elected Member of Parliament for Coventry. He died in 1865 and is buried at Edensor along with his wife Sarah.

GREAT CONSERVATORY 1840

RAINING GLASS
During the Great War of 1914-18, the lack of coal and men to look after the structure and its contents resulted in many plants dying. In 1920 it was decided to demolish the building. Repeated heavy explosions eventually achieved its destruction, with glass and debris scattered far and wide.

RIDGE-AND-FURROW
The glass was laid at angles to the main frames, which formed the 'ridges'. Rain and condensation came off the glass and into the 'furrows', made of Paxton gutters, and then down the hollow iron supporting columns.

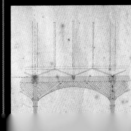

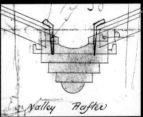

PAXTON GUTTER
A wooden glazing bar with a rainwater channel on the outside and a groove on the inside to catch the condensation. Paxton made a steam-powered machine to cut and groove the 40 miles (65km) of sash bars used to construct the Great Conservatory.

THE REVOLUTION BEGINS
AT CHATSWORTH

THE LILY HOUSE, BARBROOK

The kitchen garden was north of the house in the park at Barbrook. Here Paxton designed a tank with circulating water, which in 1849 prompted the *Victoria Amazonica* to flower for the first time in this country (page 47). Twice the lily outgrew its tank, leading Paxton to construct a tank 33 feet (10m) in diameter. This was housed in a new lily house, 61 feet long (18.6m) by 49 feet (15m) wide, which used Paxton's innovative ridge-and-furrow glazing system that he had first used in 1834. The system allowed for thin sash bars and large panes of glass which didn't need to overlap. A frame of iron beams and columns, inspired by the ribs of the leaves of the *Victoria Amazonica,* carried the ridge-and-furrow. Rainwater and condensation drained down the hollow columns.

RCHID HOUSES

1832 Paxton had built hot houses and forcing s in the kitchen garden Barbrook. Some were for hids, others for growing erything from pineapples mushrooms. Three ditional glasshouses were lt c.1834 to house more the 6th Duke's superb lection of orchids thered from around the rld.

CONSERVATIVE WALL

Also known as the Case, it was built by 1842 with striped canvas curtains and an ingenious system of flues and hot-water pipes to protect the plants. The wood and glass structure was added in 1848. The central section, originally the entrance from the park was built two years later.

Paxton's crowning achievement at Chatsworth, also known as the Great Stove, was begun in 1836 and planted in 1840.

277 feet (84m) long by 123 feet (37.5m) wide and with a roof rising to 67 feet (20.4m) it was the largest conservatory in the world and pre-dated the Palm House at Kew by Decimus Burton, who "ably assisted" Paxton with this project.

Although cast iron had been introduced Paxton decided to use laminated wood frames as they were cheaper and, if painted, would last longer. However, the hollow internal supporting columns were made of cast iron, and carried rainwater and condensation from the 'Paxton gutters'. The glass was laid in a ridge-and-furrow system, advocated by J.C.Loudon, so that the sunlight would strike t at right angles to give optimum ight and heat.

"A TROPICAL SCENE WITH A GLASS SKY"

xclaimed the King of Saxony in 843. The doorway in the rocks ed to a viewing gallery where isitors could be among the ops of the exotic and rare pecies. The dwarf banana, *Musa acuminata* 'Dwarf Cavendish' is seen bottom left.

"AFTER ST PETER'S THERE IS NOTHING LIKE IT"

wrote Lady Carlisle after the Royal visit of December 1843. Queen Victoria was taken on an evening carriage drive through the garden, which had been decorated with coloured lights. The Queen was then driven into the Great Conservatory, which was lit with 14,000 lamps, and was shown round by Paxton. Her delight can be judged by the entry in her journal "...Mr Paxton, a very clever man ... Mr Paxton is quite a genius...". In 1845, Charles Darwin wrote "...more wonderfully like tropical nature, than I could have conceived possible".

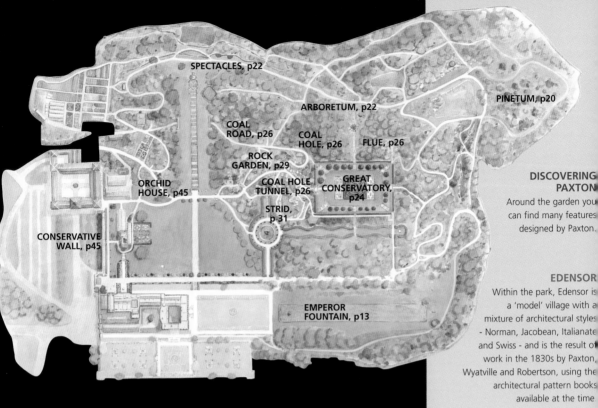

SPECTACLES, p22

ARBORETUM, p22

PINETUM, p20

COAL ROAD, p26

COAL HOLE, p26

FLUE, p26

ROCK GARDEN, p29

ORCHID HOUSE, p45

COAL HOLE TUNNEL, p26

GREAT CONSERVATORY, p24

STRID, p 31

CONSERVATIVE WALL, p45

EMPEROR FOUNTAIN, p13

DISCOVERING PAXTON

Around the garden you can find many features designed by Paxton.

EDENSOR

Within the park, Edensor is a 'model' village with a mixture of architectural styles - Norman, Jacobean, Italianate and Swiss - and is the result of work in the 1830s by Paxton, Wyatville and Robertson, using the architectural pattern books available at the time.

THE HIDDEN COAL ROUTE

Every winter 300 tons of coal was needed to fuel the boilers that heated the Great Conservatory.

Horses and carts brought coal from the railway station at Rowsley, entered the garden above the Stables and took the track [1] that went under the Cascade and on to the Coal Hole [2]. (See page 29)

From here the coal was taken in small wagons along an underground railway track [3] which can be seen from the entrance cave [4] to the eight boilers, on three sides of the Great Conservatory [5], which heated a 7 mile (11km) maze of 6 inch (15cm) hot-water pipes.

The fumes from the boilers passed along an underground flue [6], remains of which can be seen on either side of the Hundred Steps, to the tall chimney hidden amongst the trees in Stand Wood.

BARBROOK

Between 1842-7, Paxton completely transformed his cottage into this large Italianate villa, complete with tower. The glasshouse on the left has a ridge-and-furrow roof. In the 1960s, Barbrook was almost derelict and with the estate crippled by 80% death duties, it was demolished.

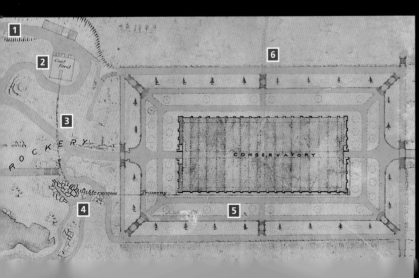

1

2

3

ROCKERY

CONSERVATORY

4

5

6

Tramway

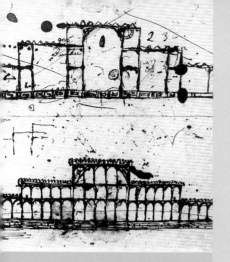

"O Paxton!"

6th Duke of Devonshire

With the success of the Great Conservatory at Chatsworth, Paxton's reputation was established and by the 1840s he was also working for other clients. His public park at Birkenhead, 1843, inspired Olmsted's designs for Central Park in New York.

After the Great Exhibition in Hyde Park, the Crystal Palace (see left and below) was rebuilt on Sydenham Hill on an even grander scale and the terraced gardens were intended to eclipse those of Versailles. Two tall water towers were built to power the cascades and fountains which incorporated nearly 12,000 jets and used 120,000 gallons (545,500 litres) of water per minute.

His work at Chatsworth and on public gardens, including those in Liverpool and Southport, as well as his ground-breaking designs for glasshouses, using the engineering breakthroughs of the Industrial Revolution, established him as the most successful and influential of the Victorian gardeners. The 6th Duke wrote that though Paxton received "...the goodwill and praise of the highest and lowest," he remained... "unspoiled and unaltered".

THE CRYSTAL PALACE, 1851

A competition was held to choose a design for the building to house the Great Exhibition. After an unsatisfactory proposal had been accepted, Paxton submitted plans based on a doodle that he made on blotting paper. At first his ideas were rejected as they were too late and the matter settled. However public enthusiasm eventually led to the acceptance of Paxton's proposal. The repetitive use of standard components, incorporating Paxton's patented roofing system, meant that this vast palace of iron, glass and wood was built on schedule for the opening of the Great Exhibition in Hyde Park. No scaffolding was needed and at one point 3 columns and 2 girders were being erected every 16 minutes. The construction took just over 6 months. The photo below shows it being rebuilt on Sydenham Hill in 1853 on an even larger scale.

SPACE AGE

A century and a half after Paxton's Great Conservatory and Crystal Palace, the beginning of the 21st century has witnessed a spate of innovative glass roofs spanning large spaces such as this one at the British Museum.

THE ROCK GARDEN
1840s

THE WELLINGTON ROCK, 1848

The apparently natural waterfall is fed by a pipe from the streams and ponds higher up the hill. The water then goes under the path to feed the Strid waterfall and pond. Every summer giant *Gunnera manicata* grow at a phenomenal rate at the base of the rock. The giant cowslip, *Primula florindae*, thrives at the edge of the water.

The Duke of Wellington was in the Royal party during Queen Victoria's visit to Chatsworth in 1843. He was so impressed by Paxton's organisation of the entertainments in the garden that he delighted his host, the 6th Duke of Devonshire, by telling him "I would have liked that man of yours for one of my generals". It appears that three large rock constructions were subsequently named after the Duke, Prince Albert and the Queen. On 13 September 1848, the gardener, Robert Aughtie wrote in his diary, "Finished the large Wellington Rock - had some ale in the evening to christen it - got rather tipsey and was very noisey coming home".

View up the Rock Garden, including the tower, which was restored in 2002.

This gigantic theatrical stage set of rocks was created by Joseph Paxton and his team of gardeners during the 1840s.

Rock gardens were becoming fashionable but few were conceived on such a massive scale; Paxton invented a steam-powered apparatus with which to move and place the giant boulders that you see. His patron, the 6th Duke, wrote "the spirit of some Druid seems to animate Mr Paxton in these bulky removals".

Paxton's aim, as stated in his Magazine of Botany, was "to copy the most picturesque assemblages of natural rocks" when creating a rock garden, and the apparently haphazard placement of some of the boulders, looking as if they might topple over at any time, was part of this effect. In the last decade a huge amount of ivy and other vegetation has been cut back in accordance with Paxton's belief that nothing should take away from the rockery's monumental effect.

◆ *Please keep to the paths and steps and do not climb on the rocks.*

A DARK TUNNEL

In 2003, part of the Coal Tunnel was excavated to allow visitors to walk from the Coal Hole to a cave entry half way along the tunnel. The Coal Hole is where, hidden from view, men transferred coal into small rail wagons to be pulled round to the boilers beneath the Great Conservatory (see page 24). Some of the track can still be seen in the floor of the tunnel. Please take great care when inside the tunnel. Admission to the tunnel may be restricted on certain days.

WELLINGTONIA

Sequoiadendron giganteum is one of the oldest living tree species dating back some 400 years in its native California. It was discovered in 1852, the year that the Duke of Wellington, victor of the Battle of Waterloo, died.

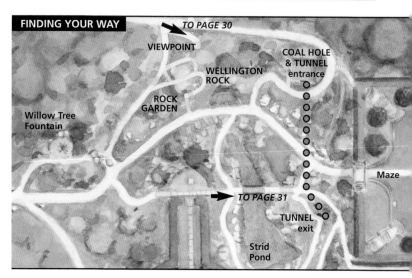

FINDING YOUR WAY

TO PAGE 30

VIEWPOINT

COAL HOLE & TUNNEL entrance

WELLINGTON ROCK

ROCK GARDEN

Willow Tree Fountain

Maze

TO PAGE 31

TUNNEL exit

Strid Pond

THE ROCK GARDEN - VIEWPOINT
2003

THE VIEWPOINT
Looking down from the top of the Rock Garden you can see the Strid, the beech hedges around the Ring Pond, the park and the spire of Edensor church in the distance. The house can be glimpsed through the trees on the right.

◆ *Please keep to the paths and steps and do not climb on any of the rocks.*

Paxton advised that **"...all the vegetation that accompanies an extensive rockery should be subordinate to it ... and to be merely sufficient and so disposed as to give relief and diversity to it'.** After Paxton, and his patron the 6th Duke, had died, fashion changed and nature was encouraged to hide as much of the rockeries as possible. Deciding that the Rock Garden should be returned to Paxton's original vision, the 11th Duke and Duchess initiated a major restoration which was completed in 2003. Part of the work involved making a viewpoint with easy access from the coal route path.

RESTORING THE ROCK GARDEN 2002-3

Paxton would have been extremely grateful to have been able to use the modern machinery available today. Some of the rocks were precariously balanced for dramatic effect. Modern legislation has required us to achieve the same effect with no risk to the visitor.

A SOLID FOUNDATION
5 men and a crane took a month to dismantle the faulty section and clear the area. It took a week to pour the concrete foundation required to ensure the stability of the rocks.

BULKY REMOVALS
Rocks weighing as much as 3 tons were lowered into position by mobile crane. Paxton invented a steam-powered machine to help place the rocks.

CAREFULLY BALANCED
It took the team a further 2 months to place the rocks in position. A viewpoint has been created between the towers. Paxton's men took 6 years to construct these towers and the surrounding Rock Garden.

The Strid Pond is a tame copy of the terrifying original near Bolton Abbey, Yorkshire, where the wide river Wharfe suddenly plunges through a narrow channel with immense force.

Here it is less than 5 feet (1.5m) deep, compared with the 30 feet (9m) of its namesake. There are brown trout in the pond. Ferns and mosses colonise the rocky edges. *Rosa Moyesii*, patches of colchicums and autumn crocus, *Rheum palmatum* and its variety 'Atrosanguineum', lace cap and other hydrangeas grow around the pond. Red-hot pokers, *Kniphofia*, make a striking show in early summer.

THE STRID AT BOLTON ABBEY, 1893
This painting by S.L.Booth shows the famous section of the river Wharfe on the Duke of Devonshire's Yorkshire Estate, where the water has worn a deep and narrow chasm through the rocks.

LOOK FOR

Acer felicifolium
Japanese acers with vivid autumn colours

Various wild, rambling and climbing roses which include:

Rosa 'Bobby James' White flowers

Rosa 'Wedding Day' White flowers

Rosa 'Rambling Rector' Small white flowers

Rosa 'Himalayan Musk' Pale pink flowers

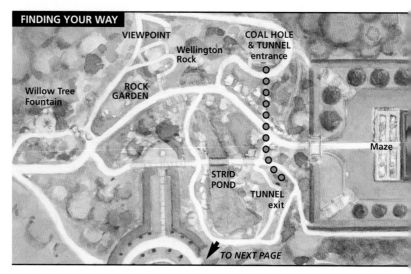

FINDING YOUR WAY

VIEWPOINT

Wellington Rock

COAL HOLE & TUNNEL entrance

Willow Tree Fountain

ROCK GARDEN

Maze

STRID POND

TUNNEL exit

TO NEXT PAGE

THE RING POND
1690s

The rocks in the middle of the Ring Pond support an ancient lead
duck, 1692, moved there from a pond which has been filled in.
Water spouts from its beak as it did in its old home, which was
inevitably nicknamed the Sick Duck Pond. There appears to have
been a pond on this site since the time of the 1st Duke and it may
have been the original setting of the Willow Tree Fountain (page 34).
The encompassing beech hedge was planted in 1953-4; beech having
the advantage that it keeps its leaves during the winter. In front, like
actors on a stage, are clipped Irish yews.

THE MILLENNIUM OAKS
2000

**43 different varieties of oak have been
planted in this area between the Serpentine
Hedge and the Maze.**

For many years this area in the middle of the
garden was a wilderness. Ian Webster had the
inspiration of planting it with the tree
historically associated with England; 'Heart
of Oak' was played on HMS Victory as she led
the attack at the Battle of Trafalgar, 1805.

BIG PIPE IN A SMALL POND

When the water is clear you can see the 16 inch (40cm) diameter pipe which feeds water from the Emperor Lake, high on the escarpment, to the Emperor Fountain.

HERMS

Herms, or terms, are stone busts set on four-cornered tapering columns. In ancient Athens they were common as boundary markers and signposts. Until they were brought here in 1893, these twelve 18th century herms decorated William Kent's Exedra in Lord Burlington's garden at Chiswick, London. One herm can be seen in the detail of a drawing by Kent shown below.

The Serpentine Hedge of beech was planted in 1953 to give the bronze head of the 6th Duke at the far end an approach of importance.

The serpentine design was inspired by the 'crinkle crankle' wall at Hopton Hall. A wall was out of the question here so beech (*Fagus sylvatica*) was used to give the same effect. The trees were 18ins (45cm) high when planted and it took 20 years' growth before it began to look right.

'CRINKLE CRANKLE' WALL, HOPTON HALL, DERBYSHIRE

Curved walls became popular after the 1784 Brick Tax. As their strength lay in the curves only two thirds the number of bricks were needed compared with a straight wall. They were also found to provide better shelter for fruit.

6TH DUKE

The bust, by Campbell, sits on a column made up of four blocks of marble found on the beach below the Temple of Minerva at Sunium, and brought home by Sir Augustus Clifford, the 6th Duke's half-brother. In the gale of 1962 the Duke's head crashed from its column in a sorry mess of branches. It was undamaged.

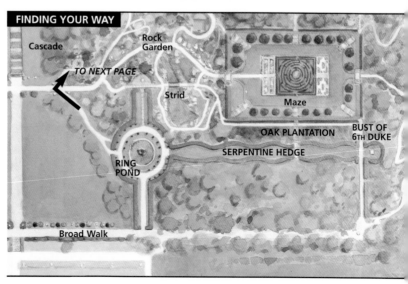

FINDING YOUR WAY

Cascade

Rock Garden

TO NEXT PAGE

Strid

Maze

OAK PLANTATION

SERPENTINE HEDGE

BUST OF 6TH DUKE

RING POND

Broad Walk

THE WILLOW TREE FOUNTAIN 1692

This fountain was first 'planted' in its own secluded little dell in 1692. Celia Fiennes, who visited in 1696, wrote:

"...in the middle of ye grove stands a fine willow tree, the leaves, barke and all looks very naturall..... and all on a sudden by turning a sluice it raines from each leafe and from the branches like a shower, it being made of brass and pipes to each leafe..."

In winter it looks so much like other leafless trees that its trick of wetting the unwary is all the more surprising. This 'squirting tree' delighted the 13 year old Princess Victoria when she visited in 1832. It has been replaced twice and was restored in 1983.

The lead statue of Pan, restored in 1991, represents the half human, half goat fertility god who protected livestock, but was also known to frighten them, hence the word *panic*.

GIOCHI D'ACQUA
Water tricks such as this were very popular in 17th and 18th century Europe and were designed to catch unsuspecting visitors by surprise.

THE CASCADE 1696-1703

The Cascade was built for the 1st Duke and finished in 1696. Six years later it was rebuilt on a grander scale. The Cascade was designed by Grillet, a pupil of Le Nôtre who designed the gardens at Versailles. In the 1830s, the 6th Duke had it taken up and realigned with the new gravel path he had built up the slope. After years of frost damage a major restoration took place in 1994-6. The engraving on page 54 shows the original Cascade, while the painting overleaf shows the extended and steeper Cascade.

When the Cascade was extended in 1702, the Temple, or Cascade House, was built to the designs of Thomas Archer. Water flows over the roof and is forced through 13 spouts, including the mouths of two dolphins precariously hung between pilasters adorned with "froste-worke". The stone carving, which includes a river god asleep on the roof, was the work of Henri Nadauld. Samuel Watson, whose work can be seen in the house, carved the lions' heads and other details. Work was completed in 1711.

WATER MUSIC
The length of the slabs over which the water flows and the numbers and widths of the 24 groups of steps are all different so that the sound of the falling water varies.

MORE TRICKS
Water can be made to spurt up though holes in the floor of the temple - another example of water trickery!

DESIGN FOR A CASCADE AT CHATSWORTH

William Kent. Pen and brown wash over pencil, 40 x 32cm. Kent's proposal to convert the 1st Duke's cascade into the 'rustic' style. It was never carried out, but a similar Kent design can be seen in the garden at Chiswick.

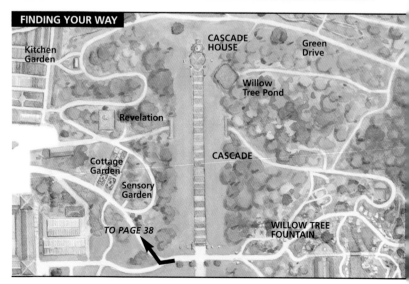

FINDING YOUR WAY

Kitchen Garden

CASCADE HOUSE

Green Drive

Willow Tree Pond

Revelation

CASCADE

Cottage Garden

Sensory Garden

TO PAGE 38

WILLOW TREE FOUNTAIN

THE EUROPEAN INFLUENCE

In turbulent medieval times houses and gardens tended to be enclosed and inward looking. This changed in 15th century Renaissance Italy with the introduction of new ideas inspired by classical ideals. By the end of the following century these ideas had spread through Europe and by the late 1600s were having a profound influence on the design of gardens in England while being adapted to suit the local topography, culture and climate.

ITALY
- NEW BEGINNINGS

Geometry and perspective linked the house to its garden and landscape.

A main central axis from the house was divided by cross axes to form 'rooms', some were filled with parterres - plant beds laid out in geometric patterns with small hedges and plants. Gardens like that at the **Villa d'Este** (above) took full advantage of their hillside site with terraces, tumbling water and unfolding vistas. By the late 16th century Mannerist gardens, full of fantasy, with grottos, rocks and water tricks, had appeared at Pratolino and Bomarzo.

FRANCE - TAMING NATURE

The flat wooded landscape of northern France allowed avenues to extend to the horizon and moats to develop into large canals. The French formal garden is epitomised by clipped hedges, long straight walks, geometric plans and an often overwhelming architectural framework.

The Italian parterre evolved into 'parterre de broderie'- swirling patterns of dwarf box set off by coloured earth and sand. André Le Nôtre designed an enormous garden at Vaux-le-Vicomte for Louis XIV's Minister of Finance. The King envied this magnificent expression of man's conquest of nature and commissioned Le Nôtre to transform Versailles to reflect his own absolute power as the Sun King. Versailles, with its 1,400 fountains, was on a bigger scale than anything previously seen in Europe. The King's retreat at **Marly** (above) where the garden was also designed by Le Nôtre, though smaller, proved more costly than Versailles. The chateau itself was the model for the West Front at Chatsworth. In the garden the long cascade of 1697-9 (see top of picture above) tumbling towards the chateau was also very influential and may have spurred the 1st Duke to extend his original cascade at Chatsworth.

HOLLAND
- HYBRIDISATION

Lack of space led to the Dutch preference for shaping nature into outdoor 'rooms'.

Daniel Marot, a French Huguenot who had sought refuge in Holland, designed **Het Loo** (left) for William of Orange between 1686 and 1695. The combination of French and Dutch styles resulted in a sumptuous garden with 'parterres de broderie' bordered by narrow flower beds. The Dutch were leaders in plant research and their gardens were used to display exotic plants - such as lilies, gladioli, hyacinths and especially tulips - introduced from the Middle East. Water also featured strongly in Dutch gardens.

TULIP MANIA

In 17th century Holland, tulips were highly prized. Blue and white tulip vases became fashionable both in Holland and in England.

ENGLAND
- AN ECLECTIC MIX

The Glorious Revolution of 1688 saw an influx of ideas from Holland and France.

When William of Orange and his wife came over from Holland and became William III and Queen Mary they asked Marot to remodel the gardens at **Hampton Court Palace** (right). The result combined the small fashionable parterres of the Dutch style with the long avenues of the French.

It was this mixture of Italian, French and Dutch ideas that influenced the 3rd and 4th Earls of Devonshire, when they began to modernise the garden at Chatsworth in the late 1600s. The 4th Earl, who was made a Duke for his part in the Glorious Revolution, was caught up with others under the influence of fashionable continental ideas that grew after the arrival of William and Mary and their court. The cascades at Dyrham Park, Stanway and here at Chatsworth bear witness to this.

This painting, c.1707, by an unknown artist shows Chatsworth when it had a formal garden in the 1st Duke's time. Many of the features seen in the 1699 Kip and Knyff engraving on page 54 can be seen more clearly in this view from the south-east. In the intervening eight years the Cascade had been extended, the Cascade House built and trees had matured. On the right is the same view today.

1. WILLOW TREE FOUNTAIN
Possibly the fountain in what appears to be the Ring Pond. Pages 32 & 34.

2. CANAL POND
Excavated some 5 years earlier. Page 12.

3. BOWLING GREEN HOUSE
A shelter built in the classical style for the bowling green in the West Garden. Now moved and renamed Flora's Temple. Page 5.

4. SOUTH or GREAT PARTERRE
1694, London and Wise.

5. WEST PARTERRE
1690, London and Wise.

6. WEST DRIVE
From here visitors walked up William Talman's steps to enter the house. The bridge beyond the drive spans the canal created by the 1st Duke from the Elizabethan ponds. The river bridge was further downstream. Pages 52-55.

7. COMPARTMENTS
The terraces to the east of the house are divided into square compartments which contain trees, fountains and statues placed to form geometric patterns.

8. CASCADE AND CASCADE HOUSE
Built in 1696 by Grillet, a pupil of Le Nôtre, it was rebuilt on a grander scale six years later. The Cascade House was added in 1703 to the plans of Thomas Archer. Page 34. Note the arches of water over each step, later removed.

9. FISH POND
A formal pond that may have produced fish for the kitchen.

10. STABLES
These are the original Elizabethan stables which were demolished when James Paine's stables were built in the 1760s.

11. FISH PONDS
Remaining Elizabethan fish ponds. Page 52.

12. 1ST DUKE'S GREENHOUSE
Built in 1698 to grow oranges and myrtles. In the 18th century it was moved by the 4th Duke to its present position. Page 44.

THE COTTAGE GARDEN
1989

The exhibit of the Cheshire Women's Institutes at the Chelsea Flower Show, 1988, inspired this garden. However it was Anne and Michael Tree's inventive garden at Shute that resulted in it taking the form it has.

'Furniture' is on two levels. The front garden leads to a living room with dining table, sofa and chairs. A flight of stairs goes up to the bedroom with 'Tiffany' table lamps and a chaise-longue. The vegetable garden with its fence of riven oak produces everything from rhubarb and strawberries to peas, beans and herbs.

LOOK FOR

FRONT GARDEN
Spring
Forget-me-nots and parrot tulips
Autumn
Dahlia 'Coltness Gem'

KITCHEN/DINING ROOM
Furniture: Yew and privet

FIREPLACE
Surround: Golden privet
Flames: Geraniums
Ashes: Grey artemisia leaves

BEDROOM
Bed, lamps and mirror: Ivy
Bedside tables and chair: Yew
Dressing table: Privet
Chaise-longue: Forsythia
Carpet: Thyme

BEDSPREAD & TABLECLOTH
Summer
Begonia sempervirens

THE SENSORY GARDEN 2004

A garden to heighten everyone's awareness of how much we use all our senses in gardens.

The Duke's son, Lord Burlington, suggested that a sensory garden would be an interesting addition to the garden.

It was laid out by estate staff over the winter of 2003/4 and included the construction of a new stream and the deliberate use of many different materials.

USE YOUR SENSES

SEE
Strong contrasts
Marigolds, sweet peas and acers

HEAR
Wind and water
Bamboos, grasses and the gentle flow of water

SMELL
Subtle or strong
Roses, herbs and scented geraniums

TOUCH
Textures
Tree barks and leaves

TASTE
Sweet and sour
Herbs

Leaving Revelation the Green Drive climbs round the Golden Grove, planted in golds and yellows, such as the crab apple *Malus x zumi* 'Golden Hornet' and *Rhododendron* 'Golden Wedding', which were given to the 11th Duke and Duchess by estate staff to celebrate their Golden Wedding Anniversary in 1991.

Above the Golden Grove you'll find the Saracenic-style Summer House, known as Luttrell's Seat, built by the 6th Duke, and flanked by the lovely *Kalmia latifolia*. In it there is an inscription from Virgil's *Georgics*. On the wall opposite is an English version, appropriate to its setting, made by Henry Luttrell in 1839.

> WON FROM THE BROW OF YONDER HEADLONG HILL, THROUGH GRASSY CHANNELS, SEE, THE SPARKLING RILL O'ER THE CHAFED PEBBLES, IN ITS MURMURING FLOW SHEDS FRESHNESS ON THE THIRSTY VALE BELOW, QUICKNING THE GROUND TILL TREES OF EVERY ZONE IN CHATSWORTHS SOIL, AND CLIME, FORGET THEIR OWN

Hidden away is the Jack Pond, which may be one of the oldest ponds in the garden. It is here that Angela Conner's water sculpture Revelation is installed.

Relying only on the natural elements of water and gravity it majestically progresses through its cycle, causing much debate as to how it works. Angela writes "The concept behind the sculpture is of a secret - first preciously held, then revealed". To find out how it works see below.

ALL IS REVEALED !

1. Frothing water fills the globe, making it heavier.

2. The globe then presses on the 'leaves' making them slowly close around the globe as it descends.

3. The water is then discharged, causing the globe to rise again and the 'leaves' to open slowly to reveal the golden globe.

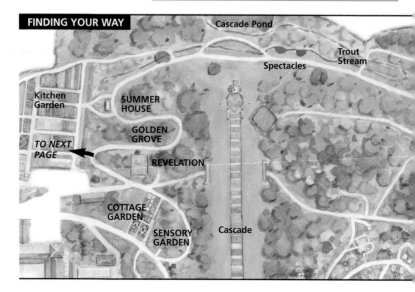

FINDING YOUR WAY

Cascade Pond

Trout Stream

Spectacles

Kitchen Garden

SUMMER HOUSE

GOLDEN GROVE

TO NEXT PAGE

REVELATION

COTTAGE GARDEN

SENSORY GARDEN

Cascade

THE KITCHEN GARDEN
1994

The seven acre kitchen garden half a mile away in the park, at Barbrook, was abandoned in 1946 and after that date a few vegetables were grown here, above the stables, in an area which used to be called the paddocks.

Carriage horses used to graze here in front of the greenhouses, but by the 1980s it was a dreary place. The three years from 1991 saw drains laid, raised beds created, cold frames restored and the whole area rejuvenated ready for planting.

Chervil, fennel, marjoram and savoury are just some of the herbs that are planted in squares along the length of the central path and the big vegetable beds are bordered with parsley and the 'alpine' strawberries 'Baron Solemacher' and 'Alexandria'. The house is now supplied with vegetables grown here and the Carriage House Restaurant takes lettuces and other salads. Beyond a beech hedge at the lower part of the garden is a small orchard with wild flowers which used to be found in an arable field: corncockle, corn marigold, cornflower, poppy and wild pansy.

THE KITCHEN GARDEN STREAM, 1998
Water that was previously piped underground was brought to the surface and now flows down a succession of features, edged by candelabra primulas, chives and *Thymus* 'Bressingham Pink' .

LOOK FOR

SOUTH FACING STONE WALL
Figs, gladioli and bay trees.

GREENHOUSES
Melons and tomatoes. Winter vegetables, such as early potatoes, carrots and herbs.These greenhouses are also used to propagate dahlias and pelargoniums.

IRON ARCHES
'Conference' pears and 'Doyenné du Comice'.

FRUIT CAGE
Raspberries, strawberries and gooseberries.

PEAS
Pea 'Hurst Green Shaft' - simply the best!

FORCING THE ISSUE
Forced rhubarb

HUNG UP
Harvested onions

LINED UP
Red cabbage is flanked by curly kale and Savoy cabbage

HANGING DOWN
'Emerald Gem' melons are supported by nets. Those in the foreground are 'Sweetheart'

SQUASHED UP
Pumpkins, marrows, courgettes and squashes

THE DEVONSHIRE ROTARY DIAMOND
Designed by Tony Pickering. Presented by the Rotary Clubs of Derbyshire to mark the Diamond Wedding Anniversary of the 11th Duke and Duchess in 2001.

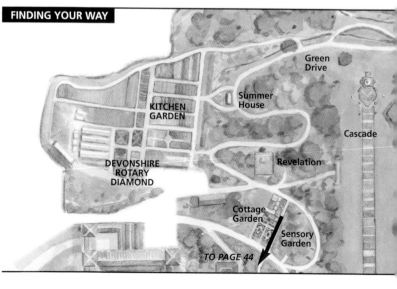

FINDING YOUR WAY

Green Drive

Summer House

KITCHEN GARDEN

Cascade

DEVONSHIRE ROTARY DIAMOND

Revelation

Cottage Garden

Sensory Garden

TO PAGE 44

FOUR CENTURIES OF FOOD PRODUCTION

Since the time of Bess of Hardwick in the mid-16th century Chatsworth has been largely self-sufficient for food.

Elizabethan Chatsworth had fish ponds, deer parks and orchards. Herbs were grown for their healing properties and for cooking. Since then there has always been a kitchen garden, but in different places. It was on the north side of the 1st Duke's formal garden (1); then in the 3rd Duke's time a garden with south facing walls for fruit trees was located south of the house near the river (2). This was swept away during 'Capability' Brown's landscaping upheavals and banished to the park at Barbrook (3). Here it flourished for over 150 years until it fell into decline as a result of the two World Wars. After the war, vegetables were grown in the area that was redesigned and opened to visitors in 1994 (4).

Weinmann, Phytanthoza iconographia, vol. 3, 1737-45

FRUIT & VEGETABLES
Before modern refrigeration these were grown outside and under glass to extend the growing season and to supply the kitchens with produce throughout the year. Today they give a supply of fresh seasonal produce ranging from the mundane to the exotic.

HEALING & HYGIENE
Like today, plants such as *Primula* and *Calendula* were grown for cooking, beauty, hygiene and healing. Many were prepared by distillation in the still room.

POULTRY
Hens produce eggs for the kitchens while the animals in the park provide meat and dairy products.

FIT FOR A KING
The menu shows the dishes served to King George V and Queen Mary on their visit to Chatsworth in 1933.

As the garden has changed over the centuries so has the number of gardeners needed to look after it.

In the 1780s, when much of the garden was uncultivated and part of 'Capability' Brown's landscape park, the total combined wages of the garden labourers was £100 per annum. 50 years later, in Paxton's heyday, the combined wages were in excess of £3,000 per annum. In 1900 the 8th Duke employed 80 people in the garden.

PAST AND PRESENT
The garden team in c.1900 and over 100 years later in 2002.

Between 1907 and 1912, as a result of death duties and the need for economy, the number of under-gardeners went down from 55 to 29 and was further reduced after the First World War. Today the advent of mechanisation has meant that a team of just over 20 gardeners can maintain the 105 acres and work with the Duke and Duchess to create new features such as the Sensory Garden.

WEATHER
Daily records of wind, rainfall, sunshine and cloud cover have been kept since the 18th century.

MAJOR RESTORATIONS
In the last 20 years Flora's Temple, stone terraces and statuary have all been restored.

FLOWER BEDS
2 acres of flower and vegetable beds are planted or replanted every year.

HEDGES
5 miles (8km) of hedges are clipped every year. It takes 2 men 2 weeks to trim the pleached limes on the South Lawn.

PRIZES
340 first prizes have been won since we started exhibiting at the RHS Early Camellia Competition in 1956.

SUNNIEST MONTH
355 hours of sunshine were recorded in July 1989. December 1930 had just over 7 hours.

CASCADE HOUSE
10,000 man hours were expended between 1994-6 to restore the Cascade and Cascade House.

HEALING YEW
In most years the yew hedge trimmings go to an organisation which makes holistic treatments for cancer.

BULBS
Thousands of bulbs are planted every year. The Duke plants many of his favourite crocuses and colchicums himself.

GRAPES
30 first prizes for grapes have been won at the RHS Autumn Fruit and Vegetable Competition since 1955.

WETTEST MONTH
Nearly 9 inches (22.8cm) of rain fell in December 1914. The lowest temperature recorded was -23°C in January 1945.

TEAMS
The gardeners are divided into 3 teams - pleasure grounds, vegetable gardens and greenhouses. There is a separate domain team to manage the park and Stand Wood.

STUDENT
Every year a Gardener's Guild student joins the team for one year's experience.

LAWNS
More than 20 acres of lawn are mown every week. We make all our own compost and leaf mould and the farms supply 20 tons of manure every year.

LENGTH OF SERVICE
The last three Head Gardeners have each worked at Chatsworth for 50 years.

THE 1ST DUKE's GREENHOUSE 1697/8
ROSE GARDEN 1939

The greenhouse was built by the 1st Duke to grow lemons, oranges and myrtles; plants which symbolised ancient mediterranean classical culture. It was moved in the 1760s to its present position, by the 4th Duke. See pages 54 & 58.

Now the 1st Duke's Greenhouse contains camellias and mimosa. In front of it is the Rose Garden, created in 1939, by Mary, wife of the 10th Duke, and planted mostly with hybrid teas. The garden was originally laid out as a formal parterre in 1812.

THE FRENCH GARDEN, c.1890
The parterre was known later as the French garden. The central stone bed is now a fountain in the inner court of the House.

COLUMNS OF ROSES
The columns, which are covered by *Rosa* 'Seagull', originally supported the galleries round the inner court of the house and were moved here by the 6th Duke in 1828.

SAMPSON SLAYING THE PHILISTINE
This lead statue, set in the Rose Garden hedge, is shown in this detail when it stood in the garden of Chiswick House.

ICONOGRAPHIE DU GENRE CAMELLIA
L. Berlèse, 1843
Camellia Rosa mundi

LOOK FOR

TREE PEONIES
June - July.
In the flower beds in front of the greenhouse.

CAMELLIA
C. japonica
'Mathotiana Rubra', 'Jupiter' and 'Latifolia'

ROSES
R 'Bobbie James'
R 'Kiftsgate'
R 'Felicia'
R 'Buff Beauty'
R 'Iceberg'
R 'Polar Star'
R 'Korresia'

Camellia
x williamsii
'Mary Christian'
prize winning bloom

Camellia
japonica
'Nobilissimum'

READY TO EXHIBIT
Camellia japonica 'Hawaii' (left) and
C.x williamsii 'Debbie' packed in a box lined
with moss ready for the Royal Horticultural
Society's Camellia Competition

PEACH BLOSSOM
The delicate flowers
produced in March are
followed by an abundance
of fruit in July and August

The Conservative Wall, so called because it 'conserves heat', faces south and is backed by an ingenious system of flues and hot-water pipes. Originally, canvas curtains protected the plants, but in 1848 Paxton covered it with a wood and glass frame. The structure is over 331 feet (100m) long and protects figs, peaches, nectarines, apricots and various shrubs from the harsh climate.

ORCHID HOUSE, C.1834
The East India House is the sole survivor of three glasshouses built specifically for orchids by Paxton at Chatsworth. It contained the 6th Duke's superb collection, gathered from all over the world (page 20). Several orchids were named after Paxton and the Duke. It is now a vinery and home to the 11th Duke's prize-winning grapes.

DENDROBIUM DEVONIANUM
One of the many orchids brought back from India, in 1835-7, by John Gibson, one of the apprentice gardeners at Chatsworth.

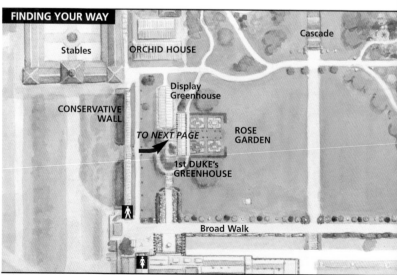

FINDING YOUR WAY

- Cascade
- Stables
- ORCHID HOUSE
- Display Greenhouse
- CONSERVATIVE WALL
- *TO NEXT PAGE*
- ROSE GARDEN
- 1st DUKE's GREENHOUSE
- Broad Walk

THE DISPLAY GREENHOUSE
1970

LABURNUM TUNNEL, 1974
Linking the Conservative Wall to the Snake Terrace is the Laburnum Tunnel which from late spring is a mass of yellow scented racemes.
◆ *Leaves, flowers and seeds are poisonous.*

SNAKE TERRACE, 1974
Designed by Dennis Fisher. The paving stones were salvaged from Paxton's Lily House, 1850, in the old kitchen garden. There they formed the rim of the first *Victoria Amazonica* lily pond. The bricks were kilned at Chatsworth c.1840. The snake, which is the family crest, is made from pebbles from the beach at Eastbourne, where the family owns property.

The Display Greenhouse was designed by George Pearce in 1970 and has no internal supports. It is divided into three sections for growing plants in three different climates: tropical in the 'stove' end, Mediterranean in the middle and temperate in the east end.

TEMPERATE	MEDITERRANEAN	TROPICAL
40° and above	**Around 55-60°**	**Above 60°**
Apricot	*Citrus mitis* Calymondin orange	*Strongylodon macrobotrys* Jade vine. 3 foot (90cm) blue-green racemes.
Camellias	*Dicksonia antartica* Tree fern	
Fuschias		Vanilla orchid Vanilla essence comes from the seed pods
Magnolia	*Datura* 'Grand Marnier'	
Mahonia lomariifolia Brilliant yellow flowers in November	*Hoya*	*Pamianthe peruviana* Sweet scented white lily like an enormous leek
	Thunbergia grandiflora	
Rhododendron fragrantissimum	The great slab of Sheldon marble, thick with fossils and quarried 5 miles from Chatsworth, was a spare for the table in the Sculpture Gallery	*Passiflora quadrangularis* The granadilla is its fruit
Sorrel Ground cover which is used for early spring soup		*Stephanotis floribunda*
		Tecca aspera Nearly black flower

PLEASE NOTE
Due to the difficulties of maintaining the climates in these relatively small greenhouses it is not possible to open them to visitors. However there are a limited number of tours available. For further information contact 01246 565300.

MEDITERRANEAN ZONE
Petrea volubilis.
One of the many plants introduced into this zone by the 11th Duke.

MEDITERRANEAN ZONE
The delicate *Solanum wendlandii* is a relative of the humble potato.

MEDITERRANEAN ZONE
Oranges, grapefruit and lemons thrive in this zone, as does an unproductive olive tree.

MEDITERRANEAN ZONE
Night flowering cactus, *epiphyllum species.* Two or three times in summer it produces up to 80 flowers, 30cm across, which by dawn have all died.

TROPICAL ZONE
Paw paw, *Carica papaya*, and mango, *Mangifera indica*, Only the paw paw produces fruit.

TROPICAL ZONE
Root ginger, *Heliconia rostrata*, (left) and the heavily scented frangipani, *Plumaria rubra.*

TROPICAL ZONE
The banana *Musa acuminata* 'Dwarf Cavendish', imported in 1829, did so well at Chatsworth that Paxton sent one to a missionary in Samoa where it flourished. It is now grown commercially around the world.

TROPICAL ZONE
VICTORIA AMAZONICA
or VICTORIA REGIA
Paxton brought this lily from Kew Gardens, where it had failed to flower. In 1849 he managed to get it to flower for the first time in this country in the specially constructed Lily House at Barbrook (left and page 25). It is an annual and still grows at great speed in the pond in the tropical zone of this greenhouse.

FINDING YOUR WAY

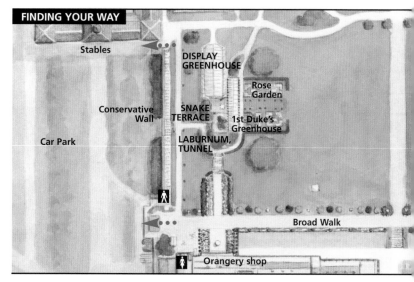

Stables

DISPLAY GREENHOUSE

Rose Garden

Conservative Wall

SNAKE TERRACE

1st Duke's Greenhouse

Car Park

LABURNUM, TUNNEL

Broad Walk

Orangery shop

In the 20th century the Library was enriched by the addition of beautiful hand-coloured floras purchased by the 11th Duke.

These include books by Redouté, Sibthorp, Thornton and recently one of the most ambitious botanical works ever published, the 34 volume Banks' Florilegium, illustrated with 738 engravings of plants collected on Captain Cook's first voyage round the world.

The natural history books collected by the 7th Duke, include the beautifully illustrated volumes by Audubon, Gould and Elliot. At the time, they were valued more for their science than for their artistic beauty and celebrated the discovery and introduction of new species.

PAXTON
Magazine of Botany, Volume 1, 1834
This monthy magazine, published 1834-49, celebrated the discovery, introduction and cultivation of hundreds of plants as well as covering more general botanical subjects. The text accompanying this plate of *Francisea hopeana* reads: "The plant ... flowered in the stove at Chatsworth, in March last ..."

PRÉVOST
Collection des Fleur et des Fruits, 1805.
La Lavatera Fleuri.
Compiled to assist designers of china, toiles and chintzes.

EHRET / TREW
Plantae selectae, Nuremberg, 1771
Detailed illustrations helped promote greater expertise in horticulture.

REDOUTÉ
Les Liliacées, 1802-16.
One of the great masterpieces of botanical illustration.

CURTIS
Flora Londiniensis, 1798.
A wonderful volume of wild flowers and grasses found near London.

Plants have provided an inspiration for artists and craftsmen for centuries.

As you walk through the house you will see in how many different ways plants have been used and depicted, whether in the fabric of the building or in a sculpture, carving, painting, tapestry, carpet, curtain, bed-hanging or in a book.

GRAFFITI
Lucian Freud, when staying as a house guest in the 1950s, painted this cyclamen on a private bathroom wall.

FABRICS
The silk from the Yellow Drawing Room (private) was copied in 1984 from the 1839 original. The same pattern, with a red background, can be seen in the Great Dining Room curtains.

A PORTRAIT OF THE ACHESON SISTERS
John Singer Sargent. 1902. Painted at Chatsworth, the oranges were brought from the greenhouse and tied onto a bay tree. Now hanging in the family drawing room, It shows the grand-daughters from the first marriage of Louise, wife of the 8th Duke. Plants from the greenhouses are always a feature of the private rooms.

WHITE TULIPS
Sir William Nicholson. 1912. Bought by the 11th Duke with his winnings from Park Top, his most successful racehorse.

A HEALTHY MIX
Seasonal fresh fruit, vegetables and herbs from the garden are used for cooking whenever they are available.

A MASS OF GOLD
Rhododendron luteum in a silver vase adorns the table in the private dining room.

WALLPAPER
Hand-painted Chinese wallpaper came in sets of about 25 strips to form a scene. Birds and flowers were cut out of leftover pieces and pasted on to add extra detail. Here we see the 'Dwarf Cavendish' banana.

ONCIDIUM PAPILIO
The 6th Duke's favourite orchid is used in the gilded picture frames in the private dining room.

PORCELAIN
Flowers, fruit and vegetables were often used in the design and decoration of dinner services and individual pieces.

THE WEST GARDEN
PRIVATE

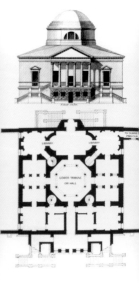

This is not open to visitors but can be seen from the State Dressing Room on the tour of the house.

The long narrow garden was reclaimed from Brown's park by the 6th Duke in the 1820s, but by the 1950s the middle section was a jumble of shrubs surrounding the Tulip Pond. In 1960, when looking at a ground plan of Lord Burlington's masterpiece Chiswick House (top right) the Dowager Duchess realised that the circle of the dome was the same size as the Pond. The design was planted out with 3,350 golden box and is only 30cm out of scale.

HERBACEOUS BORDERS
Windbreaks sculpted out of yew protect this blue and pink border which is planted with campanulas, delphiniums, lilies, peonies and roses.

GRAND ENTRANCE
The walls and busts below the West Front are carved to look as if they are covered in icicles, originally called frostwork. This was the entrance to the 1st Duke's house and was designed by William Talman. The iron work is by John Gardom.

HERCULES AND THE BORGHESE GLADIATOR
These 17th century figures, after the antique, do battle over a border planted in yellows. In the background is one of the Sphinxes surviving from the 1st Duke's Garden.

RAISED BEDS
These beds created in the 1820s by Sir Jeffry Wyatville used to be filled with bedded-out plants. In the 1970s they were replaced by the sharp geometrical patterns of box which fit in with the old golden yew cushions at each corner.

FROM THE
GARDEN OF EDEN
TO THE
EDEN PROJECT

Gardens as a place of beauty, rather than food production, can be traced back over 4000 years in Mesopotamia, which is part of modern Iraq and Iran.

The **Hanging Gardens of Babylon** were famous for their lush artificial terraces. The **Ancient Greeks** dedicated their gardens to the gods with temples situated to take advantage of the topography, views and the spirit of the place - *genius loci*. These spots were naturally beautiful and it was only in urban areas and cemeteries that planting took place.

1ST CENTURY The **Roman** leisure gardens with moving water, topiary, architectural features and statues were a combination of these influences. With the fall of the Roman Empire the necessary scientific and practical knowledge was largely preserved by the monasteries.

8TH CENTURY By now, **Islamic gardens**, with their mixed planting and delight in scents and roses, had appeared in Europe. The **Arabs** were leaders in plant collecting, identification and research, and by the 13th century had even established a botanical garden in Montpellier, France.

9TH CENTURY Charlemagne decreed that every town should plant a garden and by 1,000AD public pleasure gardens existed. The **medieval garden** tended to be geometric with compartmentalized planting, as exemplified by **English knot gardens.**

16TH CENTURY Drawing on Ancient Roman texts the **Renaissance** garden, with its subordination of plants to the overall design first appeared in Florence (Pitti Palace), but it was in Rome (Villa D'Este) that it came to its zenith. It was not long before the ideas spread north to France, the Netherlands and England.

In 1560, **Bess of Hardwick** wrote to her husband, **Sir William Cavendish**, who had purchased the **Manor of Chatsworth** eleven years earlier, *"I would have the letell garden weche ys by the newe howse made a garden thys yere."*

This is when the story of the garden at Chatsworth begins.

THE FIRST GARDEN IN 1617

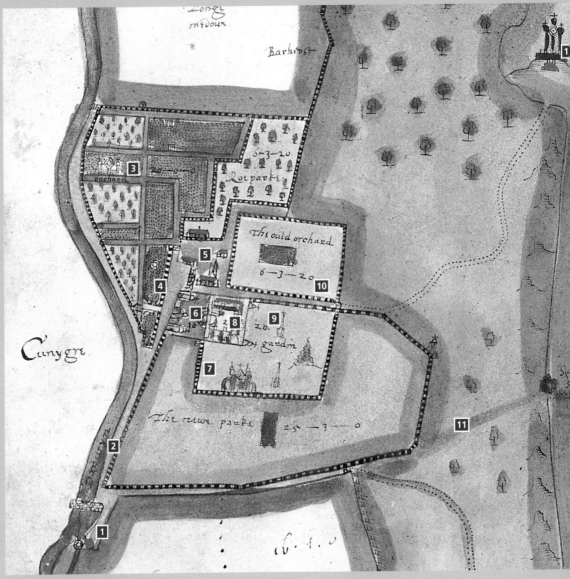

SURVEY OF CHATSWORTH
William Senior
Detail of the 1617 survey painted on vellum.

ELIZABETHAN CHATSWORTH
Richard Wilson, 1713-82
After a lost 17th century original. Many of the features shown on the survey can be seen in this painting.

AD118 - AD138
HADRIAN'S VILLA, TIVOLI, ITALY
Recreated buildings seen by the Emperor on his travels. Arranged along axes, but nestling into the landscape

1319
PATIO DE LA ACEQUIA, GENERALIFE, SPAIN
Islamic. Series of terraced water gardens set on a hillside overlooking the Alhambra

1334
SAIHO-JI, JAPAN
Zen garden with stones and over 40 species of mosses. Includes a dry garden pre-empting dry temple gardens

1543
BOTANICAL GARDENS, ITALY
The quest for knowledge led to gardens planted with rare and medicinal plants at Pisa 1543, Padua 1545 and Florence 1550

IVER BRIDGE and MILL
IVER DERWENT

QUEEN MARY'S BOWER
likely that it was first built as a
ng lodge, banqueting house or
orm from which to view the house
red in the water. It was restored in
3-4.

SH PONDS
ge across pond but not over the river.

OFFICES and STABLES

ORECOURT

HE RETAINING WALL
to create a level garden behind it,
structure still separates the South
n from the West Garden below it.

OUSE

ARDEN
ramid fountain and other garden
res can be seen.

OLD ORCHARD

ROAD FROM CHESTERFIELD

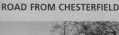

THE HUNTING TOWER
TAND, c.1582
bly built for Bess as a vantage point
atch the hunt in the surrounding
. With the formation of the landscape
in the 18th century it also adopted
ole of a folly, or landscape feature.

BESS of HARDWICK
c.1527-1608

"I would have the letell garden weche ys by the newe howse.... to sowe yt with all kind of earbes and flowres, and some pece of it with malos"

Bess of Hardwick, March 1560

The earliest reference to a garden at Chatsworth is in a letter written by Bess of Hardwick and dated 8th March 1560, eight years after she and her second husband Sir William Cavendish had begun to build the first house here.

The map on the left is from the 1617 Survey by William Senior of the estates of the 1st Earl of Devonshire - Bess and Sir William's second son - and shows the house, garden and park very much as Bess of Hardwick left them. The garden, with its emphasis on food production for the house, was much smaller than it is now. There was a formal plot to the south with ponds and fountains. The steep hill to the east was terraced and a high wall enclosed a deer park. Fish ponds were dug between the house and the river Derwent. In one of them stood, and still stands, a square stone tower now known as Queen Mary's Bower. Herbs and roses were planted as well as honeysuckles, irises, pinks and pansies. Orchards with fruit trees, gazebos, arbours and pavilions completed the Tudor garden.

SIR WILLIAM CAVENDISH
1505-1557
Bess's second husband came from Cavendish in Suffolk and prospered as one of King Henry VIII's commissioners for the dissolution of the monasteries. After his marriage to Bess, Sir William, enriched by the rewards of his position at Court, was able to purchase large tracts of land in and around Derbyshire.

1550-80
VILLA D'ESTE, TIVOLI, ITALY
erraced water garden
red by Hadrian's Villa
n was also the source
much of the statuary.
d at least four mazes

1600-82
CLAUDE LORRAINE
French painter whose
paintings of idyllic
Italian landscapes
were to inspire the
look of 18th century
'natural' gardens

1640
MOSELEY OLD HALL, WEST MIDLANDS
Knot garden laid
out in 1963 from a
design of 1640

1660
RESTORATION OF THE MONARCHY
During the Commonwealth woods were torn
down. When Charles II came to the throne,
tree planting for fruit and timber was
encouraged. Avenues stretched out into the
countryside reflecting new confidence

THE FORMAL GARDEN IN 1699

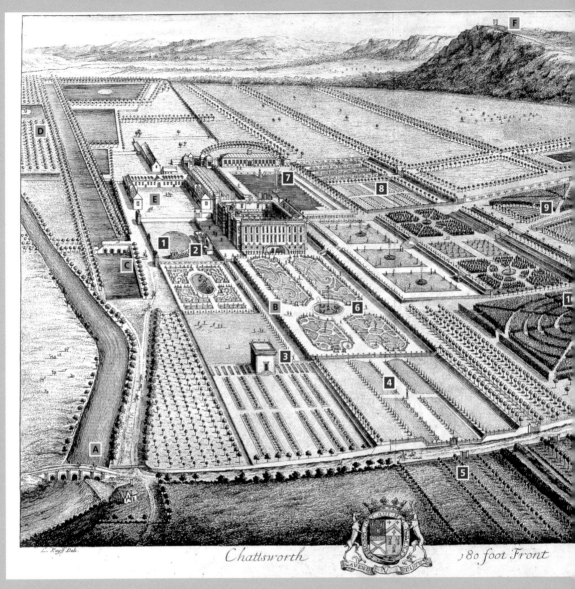

L. Kayff Del.   *Chatsworth*   180 foot Front

NEW FEATURES

1. SPHINXES
Page 50

2. BALUSTRADE
Icicles made of stone. Page 50

3. BOWLING GREEN HOUSE
4. FLORA
Combined to form Flora's Temple. Page 5

5. SITE OF CANAL POND
Excavated in 1702. Page 12

6. SEA HORSE FOUNTAIN
Cibber's masterpiece. Page 11

7. 1ST DUKE'S GREENHOUSE
Moved in 1749. Page 44

8. KITCHEN GARDEN

9. CASCADE
Extended in 1702. Page 35

10. WILLOW TREE FOUNTAIN
'Planted' in 1692. Page 34

1660
ROYAL SOCIETY
Gave a scientific basis to horticulture

1661
VAUX-LE-VICOMTE, FRANCE
Le Nôtre's great classical garden unifying architecture and garden art

1662-1700
VERSAILLES, FRANCE
Le Nôtre's grand design for Louis XIV, the Sun King

1664
SYLVA
John Evelyn's influential book which showed that the planting of trees was a valuable source of income

1667
PERRAULT'S MAZE, VERSAILLES, FRANCE
One of first mazes to tower over visitors

c.
FIRST PINEA
GROW
ENGL
The ultimate sy of a gardener's and his emplo wealth and s

1ST DUKE
1694 - 1707
WILLIAM CAVENDISH
born 1641

"...severall ffine Gardens one without another ... in the middle of Each Garden is a Large ffountaine full of images, sea gods and Dolphins and sea horses which are full of pipes which spout out water..."

Celia Fiennes, 1697

In 1686 the 4th Earl of Devonshire, as he was then, began rebuilding the house in grand style, wing by wing, to reflect his political ambition. This was achieved in 1694 when he was created 1st Duke of Devonshire for his part in bringing William of Orange and his wife Mary to the English throne after the Glorious Revolution, 1688.

At the same time as he was rebuilding the house he continued the work begun by his father in creating a series of formal gardens. In 1690 George London and Henry Wise were engaged to lay out the West Parterre and later, in 1694, to reconstruct and enlarge the 3rd Earl's Great Parterre of the 1670s. The intricacy of the patterns was admired from the elevated viewpoint of the State Rooms. London and Wise, the country's leading garden makers and designers at the time, were paid £500 for the Great Parterre and also supplied a vast number of trees and shrubs from their 100 acre nursery at Brompton Park.

The Kip and Knyff engraving, 1699, (left) shows that the garden was divided into compartments made up of trees and squares of grass defined by gravel paths. Fountains and statues of stone and brass were symmetrically placed. Waterworks, such as those here, were rare, costly and seen as a status symbol.

See page 14: Water works at Chatsworth

See page 36: European influence and the formal garden

W OF CHATSWORTH
& Knyff, 1699
lished in Britannia Illustrata,
7, showing aerial views of
y great houses and gardens
his country.

RIVER BRIDGE and MILL

RETAINING WALL

FISH PONDS
Bridge across pond
but not over the river.

QUEEN MARY'S BOWER

OFFICES and STABLES

HUNTING TOWER

1673 CHELSEA PHYSICK GARDEN, LONDON	1681 BROMPTON PARK NURSERY, LONDON	1686 HET LOO, HOLLAND	1692 'GARDEN OF EPICURUS'
Established by the Society for Apothecaries to study plants for medicinal use	This 100 acre nursery, with comprehensive stock, provided garden design and construction. Situated where the museums of South Kensington are today	Marot's French baroque garden for William of Orange	William Temple describes winding paths, wild shady gardens adorned with rough rock work

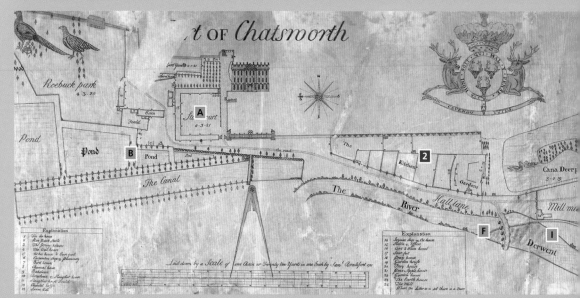

1713-8 DUNCOMBE TERRACE, NORTH YORKSHIRE	1714-38 STOWE, BUCKINGHAMSHIRE	1718-32 RAY WOOD, CASTLE HOWARD, NORTH YORKSHIRE	1720 ALEXANDER POPE'S GARDEN, TWICKENHAM	c.1725 THE FIRST 'TRUE' HA-HA ?
Grass terrace following the contours of the hill with classical temples at each end	First phase designed by Charles Bridgeman, (c.1680-1738) Royal gardener to Charles II	Contained serpentine paths, statues, cascades, fountains, pavilions and summerhouses. By the mid-18th century all these features had disappeared	Contains areas which moved away from geometrical formality	Bridgeman's ha-ha at Stowe (right) is often credited as the first one in this country, but the one at Levens Hall, Cumbria dates back to 1689

3RD DUKE
1729 - 55
WILLIAM CAVENDISH
born 1698

E HOUSE & GARDEN, c.1743

mas Smith of Derby

tsworth is depicted towards the end
he 3rd Duke's life. Much of the
Duke's formal garden can still be
n in this painting, together with his
les, the bridge and the mill (on the
t). There are signs that the formal
den was being simplified in line with
fashion for a more 'natural' looking
scape.

V FEATURES

CANAL POND

in 1702. The water jet in the
ating is the Great Fountain and not
Emperor Fountain. Page 12.

KITCHEN GARDEN

ved from the north-east of the house,
new kitchen garden had south facing
s for training fruit trees. The walls
have been banked behind for
lation. The curved wall to the right
even have been heated.

OFFICES and STABLES

FISH PONDS
Bridge across pond
but not over the river.

1st DUKE'S GREENHOUSE

HUNTING TOWER

BOWLING GREEN HOUSE

RIVER BRIDGE

CASCADE

RETAINING WALL

MILL

LAN OF CHATSWORTH, 1751

uel Brailsford

plan shows that the Elizabethan
ds and canal are still as they were in
1st Duke's time. The kitchen garden
its heated fruit walls can be seen
the river and medieval mill.

> *"...There is a new taste in gardening just arisen ... after Mr Kent's notion of gardening, viz to lay them out without level or line..."*
>
> Sir Thomas Robinson, 1734

In the 1730s a new style of gardening began to slowly evolve under the influence of Stephen Switzer, Charles Bridgeman and William Kent.

In 1733 the 3rd Duke commissioned Kent to rebuild Devonshire House, London, after it had burnt down. Kent was living nearby in the house of his close friend and patron Lord Burlington, a leading architect and father of Charlotte Boyle, who married the future 4th Duke of Devonshire in 1748. It is more than likely that there was a lively exchange of ideas between the three men. The Duke might have used the opportunity to ask Kent to sketch some ideas for the garden at Chatsworth (see page 35).

The painting on the left shows that by the early 1740s much of the 1st Duke's formal garden had been swept away in line with the fashion for a more 'natural' looking landscape. It appears that Kent's designs were not used, but his influence is certainly present.

WHERE TO SEE EXAMPLES OF KENT'S GARDENS

Chiswick Villa, London

Stowe, Buckinghamshire

Rousham, Oxfordshire

WILLIAM KENT (1685-1748)

Though described by a contemporary as "a fat and indolent man ... who talked a lot but did rather less" his influence was enormous. Kent trained as a painter in Italy (1709-19) and returned to England with Lord Burlington to become one of the leading architects and interior designers. Horse Guards, London, is perhaps his most famous building, but fine examples of his furniture can be seen at Chatsworth. Two quotes show his influence as a gardener. Kent *"leaped the fence and saw that all nature was a garden"* (Horace Walpole) and Sir Thomas Robinson's observation (above) which ends *"...This method of gardening is the more agreeable as, when finished, it has the appearance of Beautiful nature"*. In fact, Kent had little knowledge of horticulture and his garden work was more architectural.

1730-1
TEMPLE OF VENUS, STOWE
Marks the beginning
of William Kent's work
at Stowe and the
completion of
Bridgeman's garden

1730s
ROUSHAM, OXFORDSHIRE
William Kent's early
landscape garden.
A fixed route led to
stage-set type views
opening up

1735
CHISWICK VILLA, LONDON
Lord Burlington's
garden was modelled
on ancient classical ones
with winding paths and
a clear axial layout

1740-60
STOURHEAD, WILTSHIRE
Henry Hoare's informal
garden filled with a great
variety of trees to form
picturesque views over the
central artificial lake

THE LANDSCAPE GARDEN, c.1770

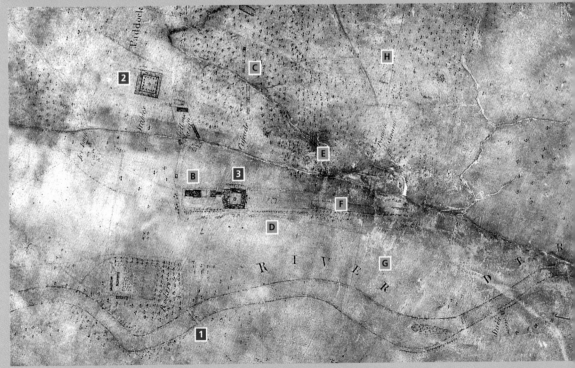

1745
FIRST SHRUBBERY
First mention of a shrubbery is at Shenstone's Leasowes in the West Midlands

1751
VAUXHALL GARDENS, LONDON
One of the London pleasure gardens. A thickly wooded wilderness provided privacy for amorous pursuits. Al-fresco banquets were served in pavilions from which fireworks and moonlight concerts could be watched

1757
ROYAL BOTANIC GARDENS, KEW, LONDON
William Chambers was commissioned by the Prince of Wales, later George III, to landscape the Royal gardens. The Chinese pagoda is one of the 'eyecatchers' in the garden

W FEATURES

PAINE'S BRIDGE
laced the old river bridge by the mill.
e new approach gave a prolonged and
nging view of the house as the road
over the bridge.

THE STABLES
lt in the 1760s by James Paine, it had
ls for more than 80 horses and
ommodation for horsemen, postilions
d coachmen. The Carriage House, now
estaurant, was added by the 6th Duke.

THE SALISBURY LAWNS

Y

HUNTING TOWER

PAINE'S NORTH WING
The 6th Duke replaced it with the
North Wing that exists today.

THE CASCADE

ELIZABETHAN RETAINING WALL

RING POND

CANAL POND

SITE OF THE FORMER
KITCHEN GARDEN
GREAT FOUNTAIN
(MORTON'S) POND

, below
PLAN OF CHATSWORTH, 1773
orge Barker
s plan shows the Cascade, the new
rse of the river and the new stables
l bridge. The Ring Pond is just visible
h walks radiating from it through the
es.

4TH DUKE
1755-64

WILLIAM CAVENDISH
born 1720

& 'CAPABILITY' BROWN

"She had never seen a place for which nature had done more, or where natural beauty had been so little counteracted by an awkward taste"

Description of Pemberley, 'Pride & Prejudice', Jane Austen, 1813

The 4th Duke made sweeping changes to the setting of the house. In the 1760s he employed James Paine to build new stables, the bridge over the river and the new mill. Lancelot 'Capability' Brown was brought in to remodel the garden and park and give them the 'natural' look for which he was famous.

Brown continued the removal of the parterres created by London and Wise, but fortunately spared the Cascade, Canal Pond and Sea Horse Fountain. The river was diverted and he removed the parts of Edensor village that could be seen from the house. The new landscaping was an immense project costing over £40,000 and involved 25,000 days of work by men and horses.

See page 8: Evolution of the natural style and page 64: The park.

JAMES PAINE (1717-89)

Worked mainly as a country house architect following the neo-Palladian tradition of Lord Burlington and William Kent. His originality increased with time but he was eclipsed by Robert Adam. At Chatsworth, working for the 4th Duke, Paine replaced the old stables and offices with a new north wing which in turn was replaced 60 years later by the present North Wing.

WHERE TO SEE MORE OF PAINE'S WORK
Felbrigg Hall, Norfolk
Gibside Chapel, Tyne & Wear
Kedleston, Derbyshire
Nostell Priory, Yorkshire

PAINE'S MILL
1761-2, was more than simply a replacement for the medieval mill. It was an important architectural feature in Brown's new landscape, an 'eyecatcher' at the southern end of the park.

PAINE'S BRIDGE
was designed to form a crucial element in the landscape.

1764-74
BLENHEIM PALACE, OXFORDSHIRE
'Capability' Brown dammed the river to form two large lakes on either side of Vanbrugh's bridge

1769-70
COOK'S FIRST VOYAGE AROUND THE WORLD
The scientist Joseph Banks sailed with Captain Cook and discovered hundreds of new species. In the following decade many of the plants, transported as seeds, became available

THE CONQUEST OF NATURE - 1858

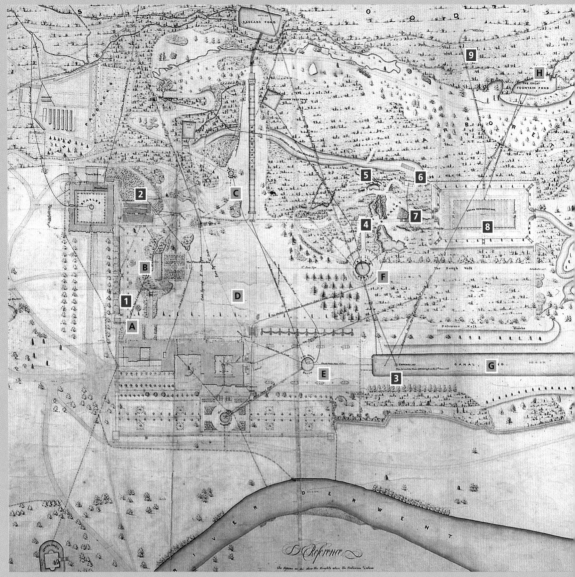

NEW FEATURES

1. CONSERVATIVE WALL,
1848. Page 45

2. ORCHID HOUSES, 1834.
Page 45

3. EMPEROR FOUNTAIN,1843.
This gravity-fed fountain has
played to a height of 297 feet.
Page 13

4. STRID, 1840s. Page 31

5. ROCK GARDEN, 1840s.
Page 28

6. COAL HOLE. Page 26
7. COAL TUNNEL. Page 26
8. GREAT CONSERVATORY,
1840. Page 24
9. FLUE. Page 26

10. ARBORETUM, 1835 &
PINETUM, 1840s. Pages 20-22

| **1759-1840**
REDOUTÉ
Produces illustrations
of plants in Empress
Josephine's collection
at Malmaison | **1830**
FIRST CYLINDRICAL-BLADE
LAWNMOWER
Man-powered mower with a
19 inch cutting blade. Pony drawn
mowers appeared 10 years later
and steam mowers in the 1890s | **1834-49**
PAXTON'S MAGAZINE
OF BOTANY
Covered everything
including the discovery
and introduction of
new species | **1836**
SHEFFIELD
BOTANIC
GARDENS
Included an early
domed glasshouse
now restored | **1840**
PALM HOUSE
KEW GARDEN
Decimus Burton
simplified the original
plans drawn up by
Turner, an engineer |

10

FLORA'S TEMPLE
The relocated Bowling Green House with the statue of Flora inside.

1ST DUKE'S GREENHOUSE

CASCADE

SALISBURY LAWNS

SEA HORSE FOUNTAIN

RING POND

CANAL POND

MORTON'S POND
Shown here with its original name - Great Fountain Pond. As its name suggests it powered the Great Fountain in the Canal Pond before it was replaced by Paxton's Emperor Fountain.

6TH DUKE

1811 - 58

WILLIAM SPENCER CAVENDISH
born 1790

& JOSEPH PAXTON

"Mr Paxton is quite a genius, for he plans out all the buildings, as well as laying out (the) gardens and the Horticultural garden."

An extract from Queen Victoria's Journal, December 1843

At the age of 21, the 6th 'Bachelor' Duke inherited eight important houses and 200,000 acres of land. He never married but loved entertaining and spent 47 years improving his houses and embellishing them with every kind of object.

He became intensely interested in gardening after he had met Joseph Paxton, a gardener at the Horticultural Society which rented land owned by the Duke near his house at Chiswick. The Duke was so impressed by the young Paxton that he appointed him Head Gardener at Chatsworth at the age of 23.

Expeditions were sent to the Americas and the Far East to collect plants. The Orchid Houses, Lily House and Great Conservatory were built to house them, taking advantage of the new technology and materials introduced by the Industrial Revolution. The Duke and Paxton also planted the Arboretum and Pinetum to show the collection of trees that they and others had gathered from all over the world.

Although people had visited the house and garden in the past, the advent of the railways saw visitor numbers reach 80,000 in 1849.

See page 14: Water works at Chatsworth

See page 24: Joseph Paxton and the Great Conservatory

See page 27: A revolution in glass

See page 28: Rock Garden

**1843
BIRKENHEAD PARK, LIVERPOOL**
Considered Paxton's best public park. Villas were designed to overlook the park

**1851
THE GREAT EXHIBITION, LONDON**
Paxton's Crystal Palace was the centrepiece of the exhibition in Hyde Park

**1858
CENTRAL PARK, NEW YORK**
Olmsted was inspired by Paxton's Birkenhead Park

**1893-1901
MONET'S GARDEN, GIVERNEY, FRANCE**
Light filled, romantic water garden immortalised in the artist's paintings

THE GARDEN TODAY

NEW FEATURES

1. PLEACHED LIME HEDGES, 1952. Page 10

2. DISPLAY GREENHOUSE, 1970. Page 46

3. COTTAGE GARDEN, 1989. Page 38

5. KITCHEN GARDEN, 1994. Page 40

6. REVELATION, 1999. Page 39

7. SERPENTINE HEDGE, 1953. Page 33

8. WAR HORSE, 1991. Page 12

9. MAZE, 1962. Page 23

1913	1920-30s	1930-40s	1947	1997
CHELSEA FLOWER SHOW Renowned flower show organised by the Royal Horticultural Society	**HIDCOTE MANOR, GLOUCESTERSHIRE** Laurence Johnston's influential compartmented garden	**SISSINGHURST, KENT** Vita Sackville-West's influential Garden with 'rooms' informally planted cottage-style	**GARDENER'S QUESTION TIME** Long-running Radio programme with a panel of experts answering questions	**GROUND FORCE** Popular television programme featuring two day garden 'make-overs'

11TH DUKE
1950-2004

ANDREW ROBERT BUXTON CAVENDISH
born 1920

"Chatsworth's greatest strength is that its owners have refused to let the garden rest on its Victorian laurels. It continues to grow and develop, and that is what makes it one of the best and most vibrant gardens in Britain."

Alan Titchmarsh, 2003

The 11th Duke and Duchess made important additions over more than 50 years. Many of the most distinctive features seen today, including the Serpentine Hedge, the Pleached Limes on the South Lawn, the Maze and the Kitchen, Cottage and Sensory Gardens were their inspiration.

Many of the classic garden stone buildings were restored, together with Paxton's Rock Garden and Coal Tunnel.

The Duke had a particular interest in bulbs, camellias and orchids. He also added outstanding illustrated botanical books to the library, examples of which are shown in this guidebook. The Duchess wrote books on the history of the garden and estate and many editions of the garden guide book.

The 12th Duke and Duchess continue to have new ideas for the development of this unique garden and the placing of contemporary sculpture in the landscape.

ENSORY GARDEN, 2003.
38

ROUGH WATERFALL, 1997.
18

ANAL & EMPEROR FOUNTAIN
ELIZABETHAN RETAINING WALL
EA HORSE FOUNTAIN
LORA'S TEMPLE
CONSERVATIVE WALL
CASCADE
HUNTING TOWER
AKES
ARBORETUM

ENNIUM
BANK,
SEX
guards
00 species
extinction

2000
EDEN PROJECT, CORNWALL
World's largest greenhouse. Plants from all over the world are housed in huge geodesic biomes

2002
ALNWICK CASTLE, NORTHUMBERLAND
A spectacular new garden by Jacques Wirtz reflecting a knowledge of garden history

2002
WINTER GARDEN, SHEFFIELD
City centre public garden with arched conservatory

THE PARK
1760s

The park was laid out by 'Capability' Brown in the 1760s (see pages 8, 58 and the park guide). Apart from the old park to the south of the garden, where the deer rear their young, the park is open to visitors free, throughout the year.

Brown expanded the earlier park by incorporating enclosed fields to the west of the river, which was widened to form a focal point and reflect the house. Brown's genius was to create the illusion of a seamless, flowing landscape that stretches from the house to the trees on the horizon. The park has always been a farmed, food-producing landscape; the grass is grazed by sheep, cattle and deer; the river provides fish and the woods game and timber.

FLYING HORSES
Each year Chatsworth commissions a leading artist to design a new sculpture which also acts as a fence for the cross-country course at the International Horse Trials. On the left is 'Pegasus' designed by Tim Harrisson in 2002.

ROYAL TRIBUTE
In 2002, to celebrate the Golden Jubilee of Queen Elizabeth II, the EⅡR cypher was created with dry-stone walls on the west side of the river. It can be seen from just north of the house.

NESTLING IN THE LANDSCAPE
View of the house and Stand Wood from the west.

PUT IN CHARGE
'Capability' Brown had so many commissions around the country that he was too busy to spend long in one place. The work at Chatsworth was delegated to his foreman, Michael Milliken; an extract of whose accounts is shown here.